THERE MUST BE A BETTER WAY

Jim Riviello
with Karen Monroy, PH.D.

LEADERSHIP
X
UNIVERSITY

Jim Riviello / Leadership X University
102 Durham Way
Lansdale, PA 19446

Publisher's Note: This is a work of creative non-fiction.

Cover Design by Asha Hossain Design, Inc.

Ordering Information:
Quantity sales. Special discounts are available on quantity purchases by corporations, associations, and others. For details, contact the "Special Sales Department" at the address above.

Visit Jim Riviello's website at www.JimRiviello.com

There Must Be A Better Way / Jim Riviello – 1st ed.
ISBN-13: 978-0615867250
ISBN-10: 0615867251

Author 's Note

The intention and purpose of this book is to share my journey to a better way. The information and stories contained in this book are based on my own experience. As customary with creative non-fiction, specific characters, places and incidents are in some cases composite examples of multiple people or situations for the purpose of illustrating my personal growth and experience. Any references to specific companies, people or situations are included for general purposes only. My co-author and I have made all reasonable efforts to provide an accurate account of my experiences and observations. It is my sincere hope that by sharing my experience, you too, will be inspired to seek out a better way for your self and/or the company you work for. Trust me when I say: "There is a better way, a more sustainable way, for all of us."

Dedication

This book is dedicated to anyone who wants to live in the world with peace and joy—and has the courage to find their better way.

"Today's problems cannot be solved
if we still think the way we thought when we created them."

— *Albert Einstein*

Contents

ACKNOWLEDGMENTS

A message from my heart

Every one of us has a journey, an adventure, and a mystery that we call LIFE. This book is intended to share with you a vital part of my journey, my story. Twelve years ago, I sensed something was missing in my life but couldn't define exactly what that something was. All I knew was that I was tired of being on an endless treadmill, tired of struggling every day to make things work, and tired of everything feeling like it was so difficult. I sensed there must be a *better way* and embarked on a journey to find it. Yes, there were times I didn't know what this journey was, why I was on it, or even where it was going.

During my search, I learned a lot about myself. I also learned to appreciate all those who crossed my path and influenced me and my thought process. Hindsight is a great gift.

As with all big endeavors, there are many people who have my sincere appreciation for their support. Just the simple act of proofreading my manuscript for the hundredth time brings to mind the many memories I was fortunate enough to have experienced. Some of the chapters made me more sentimental than I expected, especially the story about my dad, whom I wish with all my heart was still around to share more memories with me. I am forever indebted to him for his guidance and wisdom. Today he walks by my side, whispering things I want to hear, and some I wish I couldn't hear.

I have a deep sense of gratitude for my co-author, editor, and coach—Karen Monroy. I often consider Karen an angel sent my way to ensure I stay between the navigational beacons. This book would not have been possible without her endless listening and help to sort through the maze of questions I was asking myself.

A major shout out goes to my family who in simple terms, has "put up with me." You have no idea how your support and love make all the difference—every day. I thank you for your endless patience as I got my head on straight and discovered the 'new Jim.' My oldest daughter Brianne deserves credit for all her help as I began my journey into social media. Her involvement in the non-profit *She's the First* would make any parent proud and taught me to see beyond our immediate borders. Special thanks, too, goes to my daughter Abby who spent many hours editing this book, patiently offering her dad suggestions and delivering feedback in a way that defines her large heart. Her command of literature is simply amazing. I cannot wait to read the book I know she is destined to write. To my son Andrew, I want to thank you for the honor of coaching your AAU basketball team. The sport I love gave me a front row seat to witness your growth as a man, provide me the opportunity to teach you life's greatest lessons and reinforce them for myself in the process. While I pride myself in being a role model to my children, I have to admit that all three of them have taught me more than I could ever have hoped to teach them. Their sense of humor and thoughtful approach to life has been a joy to witness. Much of that credit goes to my beautiful wife Kath. What she has accomplished by raising our children will leave a far greater legacy than anything I could hope to achieve in the business world. She is the cog that keeps our family together and me grounded in reality. My love for her today is ten times as strong as it was the day we met. Thank you, Kath, for making my life so fulfilled, for standing by me when I appeared to be a jerk, and making my role as husband and father my two proudest credentials.

Reflecting back, I consider myself extremely blessed to have so many people join me on my journey. I want to personally express a deep level of thanks to all those who contributed their time, energy, and input (either directly or indirectly) to this book. Everyone, and I mean everyone, has in some way made an impact on the man I am today. Somehow the people and situations I experienced always seem to have appeared at just the right moment in my life. I have a saying I tell my kids all the time: "*Head on a swivel.*" Yes, they laugh and make fun of me, but deep down inside I know they understand. To receive all that life has to offer us, we must first raise our awareness. There is so much to learn and so many great clues and advice that are presented to us each and every day. When we raise our awareness and open our eyes, we not only see these wonderful pearls of wisdom sent to guide our next steps, but also find many red caution flags to help us avoid potential pitfalls. Whether it's business or personal, these are the moments when the *divine power of the universe* is working for all of us—the only difference is some see it and others don't. My sincere desire is to share with you my experiences and what I have learned from them with the hope that it can potentially shorten your learning curve, remove any obstacles in your path, or simply make your trip just a little bit more enjoyable.

While I do not know what the future holds, I do know that I am extremely grateful for everyone I encountered and everything I experienced. If I had an opportunity to hit the rewind switch and do it differently, I wouldn't change a thing. So many times I (we) get caught up thinking things or situations are bad, when in reality, they are all good. The BETTER WAY we are all searching for is within each of our grasps. I am living proof that it's not difficult and it's not for the special few. The secret to finding the better way is simply our ability to manage how we respond to the situations and circumstances we encounter. Maybe my story will help you, even guide you, and hopefully provide you with the courage to seek your BETTER WAY.

FOREWARD

What gives improvement, achievement or success meaning? Isn't it the growth required to improve, achieve or succeed?

We live in a world full of noise. We are all told to succeed. We ask ourselves if we are a success. Day and night we are bombarded with something outside of ourselves to buy or attain so that we can succeed.

Against the unrelenting noise of "succeed, succeed, succeed" there is an antidote in the question: "Have I grown?" Seeing the difference between who you were and who you are now allows us separation from the noise and stay true to our path. We have only one path: To grow. Change is inevitable. Growth is not. Either you are consciously growing; allowing for the foundation of improvement and success or things are changing and leaving you behind.

I've had the pleasure, the joy, and the privilege of witnessing growth in others. Some do it over long, long periods of time—others in impressive speed. Jim would be the first person to tell you he isn't done growing. But the speed at which he has maneuvered through the noise, improved, achieved and succeeded is impressive. Even more impressive is that he wants to share his journey with others. Let his journey inspire you. Let his improvement help you grow.

Everything you need to be happy, peaceful and successful you have already. If that sentence doesn't make sense to you now, I encourage you to read, and re-read Jim's book until it does.

Namaste,
Karen Monroy, Ph.D.

THERE MUST BE A BETTER WAY

Should I Stay?
or Should I Go?

Should I stay or should I go? The question is tumbling in my mind. I'm haunted by it; its shadow is cast over everything I do. I've dreamed of starting my own company since I was a little kid. I'd be crazy to leave Sun; we were—I was having the best year ever.

It was 2002, almost a year after 9/11. Recovery from the emotional and economic impact that our country endured from this unimaginable disaster was still underway. I appeared to be one of the lucky ones. A friend of mine bounced from job to job over the last couple years and was recently laid off for the second time in twelve months. As he struggled to find employment, I entertained leaving a great job at a hot technology company. My dream sounds crazy, and the lingering shadow of the dream followed me everywhere. *Are dreams meant to haunt us?*

My thoughts turn to our first quarter forecast call, and how jazzed I am to deliver the good news. My team and I are 125% of our Q1 goal. My peers, on the other hand, were not. *I looked good, real good,* I thought. I was riding a giddy feeling at the anticipation of my upcoming "that-a-boy" from my boss. *Who wouldn't want to congratulate me? Heck, I was a freakin' hero.*

Ten minutes into the call with my boss, however, all I can think is, *who needs this shit?* The focus is all about my peers and how far behind they are on their revenue goals. Strangely, the conversation morphed into a discussion on leadership and teamwork. I'm robbed of my congratulations; instead, I'm given an enormous goal increase to compensate for their lack of sales performance. My blood pressure boiled. I couldn't believe what I was listening to. My bosses' words became background noise as fury ricochet through my mind: *Is this the thanks we get for working our asses off?*

I regrouped and slowly began to make my case for why this shocking goal increase was unfair and set our team up for failure. My boss and I bantered back and forth—each volley of reason from me was countered by him. Finally, my boss leveled with me: the new sky-high goal came from above—there is no going back on it, so deal with it.

I visualized the faces of my sales team. I worked hard to build their trust and support. *How was I going to articulate this to them?* My memory flashed to my early days at Sun. I remembered the spirited and energetic times we had. The smart people I worked with and the outrageous results we delivered. Today it was not the same company I joined almost thirteen years earlier. My dream fights for the spotlight in my mind. This is not my dream. I've put thirteen years of my heart and soul into—well, into what, exactly?

There is nothing to do but let them vent is all I can think of as I give my team the news. My team is just as angry as I am about both the disrespect of overlooking our hard work and being handcuffed with this massive new goal. I'm listening to what they are saying—and how they are saying it. The *'should I stay or should I go?'* shadow is with me. I know by now, they must be thinking the same thing.

I love my team; they are a bunch of great sales people. As proof, they talk about the partner ecosystem we built and how, if leveraged properly, could help us absorb the goal increase that was so unfairly handed down. While no one likes the finishing line being moved, I witnessed a new attitude developing. They wanted to be #1. No one was going to take their hard-earned bonuses away.

Despite this setback, Q2 was just as strong as Q1. We were on a roll. I submitted my final Q2 forecast in late December. Once again, we beat our goal. In addition to a few opportunities I was committing to still bring in, I tagged a couple others as an optimistic stretch. One of these opportunities stood out amongst the others. A client had a qualified need but didn't have the budget required to purchase everything this quarter. They also lacked the space required to stage the equipment before the business was able to integrate it into production. It was Christmas Eve; my wife and I were in Eddie Bauer doing some last minute shopping. My cell rang and I knew it was about the client. I motioned to my wife that I had to pick up. Huddled behind a coat rack, my team and I architected a lease which allowed our client to get all the equipment and services they needed now, while normalizing their payments over the next thirty-six months. This allowed us to recognize an extra $5M of revenue in the quarter. Between Christmas and New Years, my team and I stole hours like common thieves from our holiday family time. When the deal booked we were all ecstatic—surely we were heroes now.

The Vice President (VP) called the first week of January. He was coming to town and requested a breakfast meeting. Quickly, I said yes. After all, who wouldn't want to brag about bringing in an extra $5M of business over the holidays? Sitting down at the hotel restaurant table I was unable to wait to hear his reason for the meeting. I began to describe the creative $5M deal that just closed. He abruptly interrupted me, and instead of congratulations, he told me how disappointed he was in me.

Disappointed—did I hear him right? Are you serious? These thoughts block all others in my mind. I'm looking for signs I'm having a nightmare—not at the breakfast table with the VP.

I just beat my forecast by $5M, which meant he beat his forecast by $5M. We both win. Isn't this how it's suppose to work? His lecture conveniently ignored the fact that I tagged this opportunity as optimistic upside, proving that I clearly wasn't sandbagging. Instead, he proceeded to tell me that I needed to improve the accuracy of my forecast. I can't remember exactly what he said after that moment as his words faded and my thoughts took over. *Was I really getting reprimanded for bringing in an additional $5M of business?* This had to be a first. While others were enjoying the holiday with their family, my team and I were working day and night.

The shadow of "**should I stay or should I go?**" is now taunting me. While I've been stealing family time—it feels now like something was stolen from me.

The Perfect Storm

The announcement came like a lead balloon: TD Bank was acquiring Commerce Bank. As part of the transaction, TD required Commerce to ensure all of their small business loans were backed by collateral. The company I left Sun to start wasn't.

The Dream?

I've enjoyed the ride, lately though it's taken its toll. *How many of the last six years have been great ones?* I wonder. I have the same "it's time" feeling I had back when I left Sun—only this time, it's my company I'm leaving and what I'm leaving to do isn't clear to me at all.

They arrived, in their suits, acting like childhood friends. We shook hands, making friendly chitchat as they offered their admiration for all we accomplished over the past six years. *We are in deep, deep shit,* screamed the voice in my head. From the moment we sat down in the conference room, it was clear the bankers had done their homework. Holding our breath, my business partner, Kevin, and I listened as the bankers slowly explained the situation, offering options that would allow us to avoid our loan being called due. In their minds, it was simple—just put up collateral.

Kevin didn't see the problem the same way I did. He actually breathed a sigh of relief. I did not. Looking at our financial portfolios, the bankers came to the conclusion that it made sense for me to put up my shore house as collateral. Out of all the assets in question, it had the most equity. In everyone's mind, except mine, this was a no brainer. They all thought it would be a short meeting. Sign the papers and move on. My mind was braking like an Indy driver just before a crash, looking for a way around the impending disaster.

My family and I call the shore house our "happy place." Something about its healing powers, the reverence we conduct ourselves with when we are there—life truly is good. Our family time there is sacred. I'd never consider risking that—besides, even mentioning signing the house over as collateral could give my wife an excuse to collect on my life insurance policy.

The business market was turning. You didn't need to be a rocket scientist to know our country was entering one of the worst recessions in a long time. One of our clients had just withdrawn a $300,000 statement of work without paying $60,000 in services already performed. The client asked us to get started before all the paperwork was signed. Kevin and I were convinced that it was merely a matter of going through the paperwork process. I questioned their history of non-ethical decisions with him, but didn't push back more aggressively. *Dumbass, what were you thinking?* I blame myself. The blaming becomes a tide of thoughts that are more and more negative. The tide turns to an undertow as I realize earlier in the week, we had three verbal agreements on significant sales opportunities cancel. The perfect storm was brewing. My boat is taking on water, and I feel the undertow sucking me under. Bankers to my left and to my right, smiling like sharks about to have a meal. I rubbed my eyes and reached for my water bottle.

Eventually the sharks leave Kevin and I to weigh our options, telling us we have a couple weeks to put up the collateral or pay off the loan. We decide to grab a beer. I felt a familiar knot forming in my stomach as we approached the bar. *The dream is dead,* I tell myself. Like a castaway lost at sea, I'm ready to surrender to the storm.

I continue the one-way dialogue in my head: *No way. Can't do it. I will not put our shore house up as collateral. Simply can't do it. That is our family's happy place. Our kids spend their summers there, working at the ice cream shop down the street, hanging out on the front porch swing telling stories, inviting their friends to visit. I promised my wife that I would never risk the shore house. It's untouchable. I couldn't even think of asking her.* The ever-present knot in my stomach tightens, as Kevin chirped in my ear how relieved he is that the company will be able to weather the economic storm. I remained silent, refusing to concur. I think the look on my face says it all.

On the surface, the credit line felt like the major issue, but it wasn't; it was just a symptom of something much deeper. For a while now, I felt things changing but I realize now I had been ignoring them, wishing they would magically go away. A few years later, when my mentor said, "Powerful people don't wish, Jim," this situation was the first to flash across my mind.

Kevin and I were inseparable when we started the company. We were joined at the hip and did everything together. When the dynamic duo took a stage, it was electric. Something changed. Not sure exactly when or where or why. We had not been on the same page regarding the vision of the company. We began to disagree on the smallest of decisions. Like an old married couple, we were growing apart. Kevin was eight years younger than me with small children. He had a different set of priorities, a stronger appetite for risk, and a larger window to recover if we made any mistakes. While he wanted to ignore the warning signs of the market, I could not. I had a daughter in college, another one knocking on the door, and a son about to enter high school. Like an investor nearing retirement, I had a shorter runway for error. My economic pressure was swelling.

After many sleepless nights, I made the decision Kevin and the bank sensed was coming: I refused to use the shore house as collateral. Our business relationship with the bank was quickly severed. The loan was called due, forcing us to secure a credit line from another bank—and quick. We packaged our financial statements and made countless visits to other banks. A lifetime of rejection was stuffed into the following month. Like an actor preparing for a screenplay, we kept pitching our story to any bank that would listen. As weeks passed with no luck, reality was slowly creeping in. Needing some advice, I called an emergency conference call with my business group. Like bees, their questions stung. "How much debt do you have? How much revenue is the company bringing in each month? Did you lose most of your income stream? What's happening to your market? What do you and Kevin agree on?" My pride answered with half-truths as I dodged the swarming bees. Justifying my defense, I spun a story of upside income potential from new markets and services I could package. At last, one member suggested I sell the shore house to jump-start the company. My heart raced as the severity of the situation was beyond the level of denial I was indulging in. I overheard the kids downstairs as a wave of nausea hit me. *Oh my God. I'm a failure. The dream, my dream, really is dead.*

Kevin and I continued to pitch our story to every bank we could find. Eventually, we were introduced to a local banker in Kevin's network. One thing led to another and soon we were back at the table, telling the story we had now mastered. Given our solid credit history, the new bank offered us a line without needing collateral. A major crisis averted, at least for the moment. We could use the new credit line to pay off the old credit line, but a consistent revenue stream was still non-existent. We'd max out the new line in months if something didn't change—now.

I went into major sales mode. For months I did nothing but cultivate my network, personally committing myself to both selling and delivering. Once again, I became a machine reminiscent of my Sun days. Working non-stop, determined to overcome. Déjà vu. It felt so familiar: the sell, sell, sell grind. *How did I get here—again? Didn't I learn anything from my experience at Sun?*

As the pipeline developed, I wanted to be optimistic—and pushed the relentless unrest I felt out of my mind. As opportunities began to close, attention turned towards our delivery capacity. Kevin and I both questioned the capability of several team members to deliver the level of service required. Instead of fixing these employee problems, I was convinced I had to be intimately involved if we had any chance of success. Eighty-hour workweeks summoned the old *"Should I stay or should I go"* ghost from the grave. I know the ghost well. After previously being haunted by it for years, I know I can't outrun it. Its resurrection has its own brand of torment as it has me replaying a question I have no answer for.

What—what should I do? My mind is constantly tinkering with, *if this happens...or that happens...then maybe I can get out of the daily grind.* These mental maybe's are on an infinite playback loop. No answer pacifies the question.

Over the following months, my travel increased. Like a flashlight in the need of new batteries, I was slowly burning out. I no longer had time to work out. I was eating poorly and usually on the run. On the rare family dinners I showed up for, my family would frequently catch me staring off into space as the daily stories were shared and bounced around the table. The remnants of me were at the table, but I was lost in the turmoil of the grind. I tossed and turned every night, keeping my wife awake as I flipped from one side to another. The space between us grew as I became consumed by the catch-22: the more immersed I was in delivery, the greater our profits, but at the expense of new opportunities in the pipeline. I needed to drive sales if this model was going to be successful. Being intimately involved in delivery froze our sales pipeline. This wasn't the dream. To me the dream of running my own company meant sleeping at night—I was in charge. I was powerful, not at the mercy of politics. I was able to turn course in a moment's notice. Do what made sense, what was truly helpful to clients. As I tossed and turned next to my wife it was clear the dream was over, but I had no idea what to do next, so each day I'd repeat the pointless robotic delivery of services and worry about sales. Still, there had to be answers, there just had to be. Something in me knew an answer existed—that much I was clear about. *How was it possible for me to be so clear there was an answer, but not have the faintest idea what the answer was?*

It seemed that while my company was struggling, other owners I befriended were finding ways to scale. I couldn't help but to wonder: *Were they sleeping well? Did they have time to spend with their family? What were they doing that I wasn't?*

Every day I would convince myself that I was a smart man. I'm a workhorse; there isn't any hole I can't dig myself out of. Others would often tell me I was lucky. They saw me having a very successful business career, a growing company of employees, a nice home, a shore house, a great family, a loving wife, and three awesome kids. On the surface, this was all good. I had all the things the world would consider a sign of success, but deep down inside I was a mess. Repeatedly, the same thoughts echoed in my mind:

THERE MUST BE A BETTER WAY, A MORE SUSTAINABLE WAY.

I continued to immerse myself further in my work, hoping the distraction would magically erase the nagging headache that was now my constant companion. The immersion was a stark contrast to the realization I needed help. More help in fact, than I ever had needed in my life. The shadow of an elusive dream is alternating between calling me and haunting me. I feel like I had come to the realization that all I had done was go full circle from my Sun days: *What keeps going wrong? Why can't I figure out how to live powerfully? Why do outside circumstances always affect me so much?*

Days, weeks, and months went by as I continued to reach out to everyone I trusted. Like a kid on a big treasure hunt, I searched for clues, wondering what I could change or do differently that would allow us to be more effective. The obvious thoughts surfaced:

- Invest in hiring a sales rep
- Fire those I didn't trust to deliver the level of quality we needed
- Create a repeatable delivery process and train others
- Modify compensation plans to drive the right behavior
- Hire a personal assistant

Yet, some wisdom in me told me that would be like rearranging deck chairs on the Titanic. I could sense others in my life were reading my mind as I thrashed back and forth, wrestling with the chatter in my head. Friends would appear out of nowhere to share an experience or mention a book they recently read and without knowing what was inside my head, the relevance of what they shared was overwhelming. I remember sitting in church on one rare Sunday appearance, listening to the sermon and hearing the priest tell a story about a child who was lost. He talked about the false belief we have that being lost is somehow bad. He challenged us to consider if the path we traveled was the one God had intended. He went on to say that only when one is lost do they reach in the glove compartment for a map. Being lost was in fact a way to focus our attention on finding our way. "How could this be bad?" he asked. Stunned, I sat there quietly, feeling as if he was talking only to me. It was like the Universe was speaking to me continually through others. *But what did it mean? What was I supposed to do? Find a map? But how?*

Shortly after the sermon, a neighbor invited me over for a drink on his patio. As we sat outside catching up, he began to share the challenges he faced with his business and how they were affecting him personally. He was feeling lost. Check mark, me too. He was searching for a better way. Check mark, me too. He spent many sleepless nights agonizing if he should stay the course or cut his losses and go to work for someone else. Check mark, me too. My pride put on a tap dance of suggestions for things he could try. Each suggestion was met by "already tried it" or "not an option." Check mark, me too. We continued to workshop question after question like two tennis players in an endless match. Refilling the glasses of wine I secretly wondered if this was my therapy session, not his.

I'm a private guy. I believe in getting help, but I was having a hard time asking for it myself. Airing my dirty laundry, trusting someone—it just wasn't for me. My never-ending question, *"Why wasn't I smart enough to figure it out myself?"* was how I reluctantly began my sessions with my new mentor/guide/teacher/coach. I had decided to "try" some sessions with her. I had danced back and forth with her for over six months. She had a waiting list, which was fine by me, because I was not yet 'on my knees' enough, as Karen would later say to me. I didn't know how much my life would change when I began my sessions with her. Truth be told, the old me would have probably run if I did. I had my own playbook for how life and business worked—you know the one that had gotten me into this mess. It had to be pried out of my hands—

looking back I can see each time Karen loosened my grip, I found other ways to re-grip the old playbook.

Like pieces of a puzzle, I was trying to connect the individual parts. Learning how to trust, learning how to be helped—to be a good student—I argued with Karen a lot in the early days. On one particular assignment she gave me I began to banter back and forth, complaining about this and that, trying to educate her on the problem, when she abruptly cut me off and said:

"YOU HAVE EVERYTHING YOU NEED, AT THIS VERY MOMENT,
TO BE SUCCESSFUL AND HAPPY"

Making believe I didn't hear her, I let my protests ramble on. She ignored my continued chatter, repeating again, in a affirmative tone: "You have everything you need, at this very moment, to be successful and happy." I found myself thinking, *"Yeah right, if I had everything I needed, why did I feel this way?"* Like a teenager with a chip on his shoulder, I snapped back: "If success feels like this, you can keep it." Surprisingly, she said nothing. The space was deafening as my words hung in the air for what felt like an eternity. Just hearing those words erupt from my mouth like a toxic oil spill frustrated me even more. I had two feet on the road to change. I couldn't turn back. I was afraid to go forward. God help me, learning new ways is so much harder to do than it sounded.

Karen would frequently remind me, "Jim, remember to congratulate yourself. You are courageous enough to admit the self-evident truth—you need a life altering change—and rightly you believe you deserve a joyful sustainable life. A new way feels difficult now because of the old habits. Keep practicing and soon your new habits will be easier than the old ones."

God, how I wanted that to be true! God, I needed that to be true.

My yearly business retreat to a remote island was one of the major events I looked forward to as a business owner. For six years I was an active member of the Entrepreneur Organization (EO). Each EO member is assigned to a forum group of 8-10 other business owners. For me, this was my virtual board. Each month we held think-tank sessions for a half-day and once a year our forum group would escape the daily routine to recharge and brainstorm different go-to-market solutions for days. Day and night we challenged each other. Surrounded by like-minded executives, my entrepreneurial soul was fed vitamins for the numerous obstacles we all encounter. At times I was coaching others on their businesses; other times they were coaching me on mine. The quiet time away became a platform to tease out cutting-edge ideas churning in our minds. Normally, I was like a kid counting the days until Christmas. Months ahead of the retreat, I would begin logging questions and ideas to share with others as I eagerly awaited the coming year's business recharge.

With our company revenue struggles, the thought of being disconnected for days weighed heavily on my mind. The clock was ticking on the new credit line, which would be fully consumed shortly. Vacations, events, and get-away meetings always seem to surface at the worst time. While this year was no exception, it also had a palpable quality that in fact felt worse.

Agonizing whether to attend or not for weeks, I put the question to Karen. "Should I go?" She asked me to articulate how it felt to go. When I finished with my twisted rationalizations about why I shouldn't go, Karen asked me again, "So it feels disturbing when you think about going?"

Well duh, I think I just said that. I felt short as I smothered the thought—*"be cool,"* I pridefully told myself and asked, "So you think I should cancel?"

Before I could begin to counter with the cons of canceling Karen gave me the homework to write the pros and cons of canceling on a sheet of paper, drawing a line down the middle, each pro would have a corresponding con, she said. Just open up to the process, Karen said—don't try to steer the answer.

After going through the homework assignment it was clear to me I needed to cancel. I heard myself share this with Karen, telling her I knew it was the right thing to do—and then she asked me, "Why?"

"What do you mean why? I thought you'd agree with me."

"My agreement isn't even the point, Jim. It's not my life; it's not my decision. I want you to use the principle of Clarity. Be clear about why it's the right thing for you."

I stumbled like a blind man in a new environment, tossing out answers before it occurred to me to be honest: "I don't know why," I said, somewhat challenging her.

"Okay, I'll give you this one, Jim," Karen said with a light hearted hum in her voice "It's over. Your run with your company is over. Your bags are packed; you are at the train station waiting for your train to pull out of the station. It doesn't make sense to brainstorm how to resurrect a company you have mentally left."

My knees buckled. My spine tingled.

"Does that resonate with you?" Karen asked

"I can't explain what I'm feeling, but yes, yes, yes it resonates with me like you'll never know."

"So the decision to not go on the trip is just the precursor to announcing the bigger decision?"

"Yes, it is," I concur.

"And even though the big decision seems hard, you feel at peace with it?" Karen asks.

"Yes, I do—and no I don't," I tell Karen. I go on to list how hard it will be to let Kevin know. How it will look to others, how my wife will worry....

"Jim, just stay with the Peace. Don't jump forward with the how or what's next. Open yourself to the help that is available, that will come your way once you are clear about the 'what'."

As I canceled my trip, my moments of clarity seemed to fade. I went back to my pro and con list and focused on my number one pro: "To focus on much needed revenue." Kevin and I were in separate forum groups, each attending different retreats. Somehow I assumed he would cancel his trip as well. I was wrong.

The chatter roared in my head: *What was I thinking? How could I have been so naïve to think he would? Why didn't I see this coming?* I couldn't shake the thunderous voice in my head. As if I was a lawyer trying to convince a jury, I caught myself arguing my case as a victim on my daily commute home. Sadly, I was the only one in the car. To be honest, the trip wasn't the only situation that infuriated me. I became more and more disappointed in myself for the additional sacrifices I was making.

I didn't think God intended everything to be this hard. To make matters worse, I was further complicating everything with my own refusal to consistently accept the reality of the situation. This is one of the first principles my mentor was teaching me: See it clearly, whatever "it" is, and say what it is. "Think of all of the energy you have spent avoiding this situation, Jim," Karen said. "When you decide to accept the situation is no longer working for you, your energy can be spent on moving forward. Until then, this jumping in and out of denial and acceptance is what is disturbing your Peace—not Kevin."

Some days, I was doing my best to ignore many of the warning signs the Universe was sending. Other days lumbered on. Each segment of the day was a constant reminder—my ninety-minute commute to work, the weight of company sales and delivery, and the constant disagreements with Kevin were aging me like dog years. Exhausted from running on this endless treadmill, I caught myself silently praying for it to all stop.

With anxiety mounting, my mentor, Karen, pushed me to reach out to my network—again. "Trust," she said, "The Universe wants you to succeed. Most people don't realize the single most important decision they will ever make is if they live in a friendly Universe or an unfriendly Universe. If you were meant to stay and make the company work, you would be at Peace when you think of that. Do you feel Peace when you think of staying?"

Ugh. No, I felt no Peace. There was no denying that.

I gathered the courage to confide in a couple of my closest clients. Their reaction came as a welcome relief. It wasn't long before the conversations revealed numerous employment options, a clear indication that the relationships I built over the years were genuine. Within weeks, three great employment opportunities crystallized, each having an attractive financial package. Not knowing which one I would eventually pursue, I approached Kevin to let him know I was leaving. I offered different exit strategies for the two companies we collectively owned to ensure a smooth transition. As the ultimate optimist, he attempted to talk me out of it, desperately trying to convince me that it was about to get better—the same lie I had been telling myself for years. He was a Marine and a Marine weathers the storm. I knew there had to be a better way, and it wasn't to be found by staying.

Instead of being relieved and enthusiastic about the multiple options in front of me, I had overwhelming anxiety. On one hand, I was filled with excitement. On the other, I was secretly scared to death. *How ironic,* I thought to myself. *My dream is now to get out of my own company.* I was tormented by the idea of going to work for someone else—back and forth the desperation to save myself, and the desire to stick with it continued. "The jumping in and out of denial and acceptance." Karen called it.

This company was my baby; I incubated it and led its growth but the Universe keeps sending me signs that I need to go. *Was Kevin right? Should I fight through this? What would others think if I didn't? How would our employees and clients react if I left? What would my circle of family, friends and neighbors say? Would this be a quiet relief to my wife or yet another disruptive change? As a role model, what message would I send my kids?*

"You know the mind will always tell you the unknown is bad," Karen reminded me. "You have plenty of proof the current situation is bad, Jim. Let's work on straightening out your thinking so the real you is in charge of your life."

I called a friend of mine, Dave, a successful entrepreneur in my business group, hoping he'd have another option other than to save myself or help me feel better about leaving. Dave proceeded to tell me a story of a pilgrim who boarded the Mayflower with the promise of a better life in America. Halfway there, a violent storm broke out. On the verge of turning back, the crew repaired the damage and plugged the leaks caused by the unforeseen weather. When the storm passed, the pilgrim realized the ship was blown off course. Needing fresh water and supplies, they were forced to make a stop in Newfoundland before setting sail again to their ultimate destination. As he concluded his story, he paused and said: "Jim, I think of you as that pilgrim." Ah, yes. The Universe uses everything for my good, as Karen was teaching me. *So maybe the dream isn't dead—maybe, just maybe I need to make a stop in my personal Newfoundland?*

Over the coming weeks I narrowed my employment options down to two. One of them was a current client. We met at Starbucks to review the details for becoming their Chief Operating Officer (COO). They wanted me to be a strategic member of their executive management team and lead the overall growth of the company's business model. I had started working with them when they were a small $3M company with a couple of employees working out of their homes. Now, at the time of this meeting, they were a $13M company on the rise. Over the previous months, we had brainstormed different approaches to double their growth. While most consultants are regarded as pie in the sky thinkers, they challenged me to become their COO and put into practice everything I recommended as part of their growth strategy. I weighed the pros and cons. The thought of working for someone else definitely concerned me but the challenge of helping them get to the next level was extremely intriguing. I contemplated the difference of driving change within a company as opposed to the influence a consultant provides. *Would others embrace the adjustments I had in mind? Would I?* It was the beginning of a desperate, round-the-clock attempt to find out.

The Beginning of New Beginnings

I entered the building, approached the elevator, and anxiously took the short ride to the 4th floor. "So this is it," I whispered to myself as I opened the glass doors. New job. Working for someone else. *Dear God, let this new job be great,* I silently prayed as I extended my clammy hand to introduce myself to the new faces. The introductions were short, as was the demo of the sophisticated phone system. My MacBook was like a strain of bacteria unleashed into the Microsoft environment of the new office. I could sense others were watching me closely, inspecting my every move. "Leadership is earned, not granted," is the mandate I received from Frank, our CEO. *Can I earn their trust and respect?* Their faces were hard to read.

The first month was awkward. I made my rounds converting the new faces into team members. I searched for thoughts, opinions, ideas and suggestions. Smart people everywhere—I like that. Entrepreneurial culture—liked that too. No discipline. Minimal leadership. Like firemen, everyone was skilled at reacting to the drill of the day. I don't like that. The smart ones were so good at fire drills that it was the norm. I really don't like that. Success had come quick, but a formula for long-term sustainability was lacking. I knew it. Frank knew it too. "I brought you in for a reason," he said. "You have the skills to do what I cannot. We need a factory of repeatable processes that will define our culture, diversify our client base, and allow us to scale." My mission was clear—or so I thought.

The only official salesperson was the guy I met on my first day. I lied when I shook his hand and said, "I look forward to working with you." I had already been forewarned before accepting the position: he wasn't a sales guy. He had to go, and quick. Marketing was non-existent. The wild, wild west decision-making behavior made it difficult to garner support for the processes we desperately needed. I was shocked to discover that the CFO, Sam, lacked the trust of those who counted—including me. All this needed to change, and fast.

"When in doubt, just attack." It was a mantra my father gave me as a college freshman to overcome the doubt plaguing me about my academic ability. Time to get out my playbook, roll up my sleeves and make it all happen.

"But aren't you looking for a better way?" Karen asked me when I had laid out my grand plans. "So you want a new treadmill? I thought you wanted to get off the treadmill?"

I had been working on peace of mind. Establishing sacred time for myself to reflect, be, breathe. Mostly in this sacred space I was trying to catch the fleeting wisdom I was beginning to get glimpses of. I was beginning to respond to others differently. "Don't feed the frenzy," Karen reminded me. She sensed I was about to dive deep into my work, work, work mode again and was trying to warn me against my overzealous habits. I was making progress—I knew it, and so did she. Through practice, I was learning that I was truly responsible for how I show up; no one can make me crazy unless I give them permission. Regardless of how much I tried, this theme kept resurfacing.

Karen and I often laugh now about the time she pushed me for weeks to turn off my email notifications. "Jim, this is something you can try. Set your email to download every hour—not when it comes in. Try it for a day. What is the worst that can happen?" My list of the worst that could happen was long. And to each item on the list she reminded me I had some new skills to handle whatever it was and keep my peace of mind. With trepidation, I decided to turn off those nasty little pop-ups every time a new email arrived on my laptop. Turning off the alerts on my iPhone was just as challenging. I kept the email setting for the entire week. When I reported back the next week, "I can't believe how much actual work I got done! How productive I was—I don't believe it!" Karen said, "Just think how much easier your days would be if you had done that sooner. It's called ease and grace, Jim. It's always available to us. We receive it when we are willing to change."

The next twelve-months flew by as I worked diligently on laying the foundation for the exceptional growth to follow. As a management team, we established a growth plan that everyone rallied around. Slowly, our culture was beginning to evolve. I challenged others to imagine the company twice its size and invited them to propose the support required. Believers were beginning to emerge from the efficiency gained through greater discipline. As our sales, technology, and recruiting team grew, so did the acquisition of new accounts. It was electrifying. A new level of confidence caught fire throughout the organization. Inc. 5000 recognized us as #788 at a time when other companies were declining. We landed at #12 on the Philly 100 and made the Future 50 Emerging Companies in the Mid-Atlantic region. Large technology vendors like Microsoft, Oracle, and Symantec were now calling us. The company was on a roll and so was I.

Frank wanted everyone to be happy. This was his most endearing quality and one of his biggest challenges as a leader. Seeing himself as a 'man amongst the people,' he strived to make others feel special, believing this would motivate them to do more. Growth ushered in a new set of problems. In closed-door sessions, individual contributors began to demand more money—unfortunately, not with their immediate manager. Aware of these sessions, I braced myself for a crest of problems experience told me was certain to follow. Not everyone gets the VIP package. Everyone thinking they can have one creates a very slippery slope.

With frustration, I watched employee after employee put on their best act, enter his office, each bringing with them their own set of demands. The wild-west decision-making reared its head again and again. Impulsively, Frank modified compensation plans to satisfy individual demands. A breeding ground of prima donnas emerged and "me, me, me" was their mantra.

One Saturday, I came downstairs early, wearing my favorite baseball cap and sweatpants, brewed a fresh pot of coffee, and energetically anticipated a great day. I'm just learning how to savor the moment—to unplug. The unrelenting question of "what's happening at work?" is my competition for unplugging. The mere query of this creates anxiety. Usually it's a repetitive series of self-inflicted craziness that convinces me that I have to know what is going on. *What requires my attention? Who needs me? What damage control do I have to do?* I tell myself that I really don't want to know—but secretly, I wonder if I do. Every device and gadget I have is geared to perpetuate this elusive answer.

My son had the second of three basketball games that weekend. My goal: catch up on a few items before the basketball games began. Get in—get out—done. Sounds simple. What I didn't realize is the short drive to crazy had already started. Fifty new emails appeared in my inbox, another hundred on their way. *Damn it! Why the heck did I check email? Shit!* It's all I can think. I KNOW BETTER. I know Karen is going to tell me in our next session, "You can't betray yourself and expect not to suffer." Damn, damn, damn.

Immediately I was sucked into the vortex of electronic mail. Karen is fond of telling me when I need to practice a principle; I'll get plenty of chances. "It's just how the Universe works for our good," she says. Creating space. That's been my homework. I keep getting opportunities to practice but don't sense them until it's too late. *Shit!* Space, Karen was telling me, is my job. "No one controls your day but you, Jim. The illusion you have now is that someone else does." I wasn't practicing the principle of creating space.

The day before, one of our employees, Alex, resigned. This ignited a series of emails, meetings, and an extraordinary amount of drama. Help was solicited from senior members of our organization. Like little elves, everyone scurried to workshop messaging as to "why" Alex was leaving. Now, I know what you're thinking—Alex must have been pretty valuable. While every employee is important, Alex and the company were not always on the same page. Alex was extremely talented, but for a variety of reasons, struggled to build rapport with others in the organization. He came from a large organization and often clashed with the mentality of an entrepreneurial firm. Alex's role within the organization changed a half dozen times over the previous six months, which ultimately led to his resignation. While he had a couple of nice opportunities in the pipeline, his account base was small and his success limited. One could imagine that a transition plan for Alex would be rather easy. Instead, the tension resembled a White House scandal about to be leaked on CNN. Emails flying every which way: "What should we do? Who will take what account? How should we position this to our clients and partners? What message do we give our employees?" Similar to an instant messaging chat session, everyone offered his or her two cents. I couldn't react fast enough. Amongst this flurry was an email from Frank letting me know he scheduled meetings with Alex to transition his accounts. Scanning further, I didn't see any calendar invites. This was just the latest in a long line of behaviors from Frank that was undoing what I had been working so hard to build—the discipline to avoid the drama and fire-fighter mode we previously engaged in. A pulsating pain germinated from my temple. I reached for what was now a cold cup of coffee. Once again, I heard the familiar voice cry out:

"THERE MUST BE A BETTER WAY"

A Willing Student

"I want to write a book," I blurt out to Karen at our annual review. She smiles and hands me her new book. I'm constantly commenting on her uncanny nature to be in sync with me. She presents a theme for a lesson in our weekly session—and it will be exactly what I had been thinking about. I'm trying not to be unnerved by it, but frankly at times I am. I wonder if she can read my mind.

"Okay," she says, "I think first we ought to get serious about your practice." Uh-oh. I know the tone in her voice. I joke that I am a little grasshopper, struggling to learn to do things differently—but more importantly to see them as they really are, not how my habituated mind sees life.

Karen reviews my progress. She speaks of my successes, areas she has seen I've grown. I feel I've grown too. Significant changes in the area around being reactive to people and situations are noticeable. We've worked hard on a peaceful ground of being. It's the foundation for everything else. While I intellectually get that my peace is not dependent on others being different, or situations being different, in practice I'm still a little grasshopper. Internally, I know it and sense she does too.

"You really need to ask yourself, Jim, if you are willing to apply yourself. You are getting results, but not nearly the results you could get if you made the decision to be a good student." I hold my breath—no one ever told me that. She tells me to breathe. Karen once again talks about resistance. She asks me to let my guard down, not to her, but to the goodness of life. "Not only are you so hard on yourself—always trying to be perfect, always trying to do things 'right'—you have not yet decided that you live in a friendly Universe. Life loves you—you must love it back. Guarding against what it could bring interferes with that."

"Resistance," Karen hums the word, "is normal. It means you are normal. Fooling yourself that you are doing the work—that's also resistance. Coming up with excuses as to why you haven't done all of your homework each week—that's normal resistance too. My question for you is this: do you want to be normal?"

I'm speechless. Hell no, I don't want normal. I've had enough of normal, but I think she is being too hard on me. I always considered myself to be a good student. I protest, with a challenge: "Okay, tell me what you think I'm not doing." She smiles. Instantly I know the little grasshopper is about to be schooled.

"Let's look at your quiet time and journaling," she says. "How far did I have to put my foot up your butt before you agreed to take five minutes of quiet time each morning?" I smile and think about how hard that was for me. I refused to try it because I didn't see the merit of doing it. I reluctantly capitulated when she slayed my latest 'I really don't have time' excuse with, "If you tried earnestly for just one week, Jim, what's the worst thing that could happen? You'd lose thirty-five minutes? You mean you can't spend 35 less minutes on email drama to benefit yourself?"

Karen thoughtfully squeezes the lemon into her water; she takes a sip, slowly punctuating the silence. She knows I'm not going to answer as she continues, "You just may discover that you can train your mind to 'not think' which is the beginning of an inner peace you have never experienced. Your creativity is fed by willingly expanding your quiet time—how consistent are you with quiet time?"

I smile again and offer my earnest "fair enough, point taken."

"And when you journal, isn't your experience that you actually see deeper into circumstances and situations? What wasn't clear becomes more clear?" Before I can offer my answer she finishes her comment. "And yet, despite all the evidence in front of you, despite your own experience with the benefits you are not consistent with these tools."

I know everything she says is true. I feel frustrated and quip, "How do I get consistent?"

"Ah, little grasshopper," she laughs, "now you are asking a meaningful question. Can you feel deep within you the difference between doing something to gain a benefit and doing something out of complete **Trust and Surrender**?"

I have to catch my breath. Over the last few weeks, each time I prepared for my review these two words came to me. I'm afraid to say this out loud to her when it occurs to me she already knows. "How do you do thaaaaat?" I query her, unable to contain my amazement.

"That's not a very good question."

My mind is going in circles searching for a good question. "It's about Trust and Surrender?"

In her best Kung Fu accent comes, "Very good little grasshopper." She's laughing.

I join her with my laughter, feeling like I have uncovered a hidden gem. Over my laughter she says, "That's the difference between you and me right now, Jim. I made the decision to **trust** the goodness of life a long time ago. I decided my way wasn't working sustainably so I have chosen to **surrender** to the Universal way that does."

"I want that!" I exclaim cutting my own laughter off. "I want that," I repeat.

Karen takes a long, slow, deep breath. She sits back in her chair, her eyes searching mine. "I have two things to say to your request: the first is you need to be a better student—a willing student."

"I know," I say softly. "I know."

"Isn't it a relief to finally be honest with yourself, to be in integrity with yourself?" she asks. There is no denying it. I feel what I feel. This feels right, in every fiber of my being it resonates.

"The second thing I have to say," she continues, "is you must give very, very careful consideration to your request to learn Trust and Surrender. Trust and Surrender are a gateway to incredible internal power and they come with great responsibility. I want you to think about this before you decide. People can get very afraid of being powerful. And most of all, if you are not a willing student, Trust and Surrender will feel like a two-by-four between the eyes."

There's a shift in the energy at the table. The hair on the back of my neck is at attention. I look around the room to see if anything is going on in the restaurant. Everyone else seems to not notice, but I do—there is an electric presence in the room. Some kind of mystical invitation has been issued and I can't quite take hold of it.

"It's a door, Jim," Karen informs me. "It will stay open for you, so no need to hurry through it. Your choice right now is do you want to learn with ease and grace, or do you want to learn on your knees?"

I mumble back to Karen one of her mantras, "We never get to pick the lesson—just how we learn it."

'A-plus little grasshopper, A-plus."

The shift in energy is staying with me as I cross the bridge spanning the Delaware River. I feel the door life has opened to me. I sense I will need, more than ever, my gratitude list. I observe I'm inconsistent with this tool too.

I play back part of my conversation with Karen: "Every tool has but one purpose, Jim—to change your perception so you can change your mind about how things really are. All authentic personal power is built upon a peaceful mind that can see rightly." I pull over and look at the river. It's moving, but it's peaceful. The current has ease and grace—it has power. I have a thought that I know is trying to hook me. I can see the resistance my mind—my monkey mind, as Karen calls it—is trying to stir up. It's so simple, I think, smiling to myself. It's just like the river. I can move the thoughts along—peacefully, quietly. I don't have to make a home for them in my head. I sit for hours by the river, adjusting to the new door life has recently opened for me. I'm mostly processing the power of Karen's words: *Do I want to be normal? Do I want to learn with ease and grace? Am I afraid of my own power? Can I Trust? Can I Surrender? Can I let my old playbook on life go and be a willing student?*

As I walk back to the car, my eye catches the road ahead. The country fall foliage is vibrant and picturesque. I have always been fascinated with roads as if they weave a certain mystery. I see the bend ahead and the passing car vanishes from sight. I have no idea where my journey is leading me or what lies around the upcoming bend. I do know for certain that it is definitely a road trip I must take. As I begin my drive towards home, I hear Karen's voice and replay a story she shared with me, "When I was a girl a man asked my father about his secret to success. I was instantly captivated by the question, I had no idea there were people who were not successful. His answer has stuck with me all these years: "Life is like poker," he said. "You can either play to not lose or you can play to win. I play to win."

"I'm playing to win," I exclaim at the start of my next phone session with Karen. "No more playing to not lose."

"Well, then. Let's get serious."

"Why do I feel like I'm about to regret my decision?" I say half jokingly.

"I promise," Karen says, "everything you do you will be able to test and verify for yourself that it works—but you have to do the homework, all of it, with your whole heart, with Integrity."

"Okay, I'm all in," I declare. Instantly I feel as if I have stepped through a door. I haven't been this excited about life, about its possibilities in, well, I don't remember since when. The energy is back; I recognize it and fumble with words as I try to describe it to Karen.

"Let's put the energy to good use: the first homework assignment of the new you is to draft your first blog post. You want to write a book so you need to start sending your energy in that direction," she says.

"I was just thinking about writing a blog! And to demonstrate I can be a good student, I won't even tell you any excuse I have as to why I can't."

We are both laughing now. "Good," Karen says. "Because that is also the first rule of the new you. You must accept the responsibility of the choices you make. There are no excuses—only choices. You are going to use this tool all week. You are not allowed to give a single reason why. No defending, rationalizing or minimizing. You make a choice, and either it works or it doesn't get the results you want—either way your choice must be no excuses."

"The new me?" Silence. "The new me," I affirm. "The new me is excited," I tell her.

"Good, because the second homework assignment you have is to write down every excuse the old you wants to make."

"Does anyone ever tell you how much they love you and hate you at the same time?" I say with a chuckle. She doesn't need to answer; I can feel her smile. "You have a great week Jim, I'm excited for you. Welcome to your new life."

As I hit the end call button on my cell phone, I can feel it again. The energy is palpable. Something has changed. I can't name it, but I sure can feel it. It feels like I am finally on the right road—the road to home.

The Man in the Mirror

"Dad, maybe if you stand on one leg you'll get a bar."

"See, it's a sign you are not supposed to be working!" my wife, Kath, yells from across the room. "Stop trying to call the office!"

The comments continue as I silently fume at the Universe foiling my attempts to violate my promise to unplug from work during my vacation. What is it that Karen tells me? "The Universe in its loving wisdom holds you to your promises?" I promised myself, Kath, and my kids that I would disconnect—I think I even gave Karen some line like, "No problem, sign me up! I'm ready!"

I had the best of intentions. Really. My homework was simple: unplug for the entire vacation. When Karen challenged me with "Are you ready to make the commitment to yourself?" My insides screamed, "Hell YES!"

My in-laws were celebrating their 50th wedding anniversary. We were all meeting at a house we rented in the Adirondack Mountains. Kath's entire Irish family was there—all nineteen of us together for a week.

Somehow I thought wanting to unplug was enough. I had the willpower, the motivation. I had been deepening my practice of alignment with the life I want—which decidedly did not include being plugged into an office 24/7.

Yet, despite my yearning to keep my promise I can't suppress the feeling that I need to check my email. The itch is creeping over my entire body like a bad case of poison ivy. I simply will go nuts unless it's scratched. I begin my rationalizations, "*One quick look. I won't even answer anyone. I will be able to relax much more if I know everything is okay back at the office."* I actually notice the excuses I am making. I make a note to tell Karen about this improvement—noticing the monkey mind in the moment.

What sacrifice would the gods demand from me for violating my word? Maybe I can pay the price? The thought scares me. This is not a good student moment.

I'm grasping for something to ground my mind. It's being pulled relentlessly towards the temptation to check email. And then, mysteriously, a conscious decision to check the email—damn the price to be paid, I'm checking it.

Within moments I'm hooked. More problems are spiraling out of control, out of *my* control to be more precise. Another mess for me to clean up when I return. *"Okay,"* I rationalize, *"just a few quick phone calls and I will nip this in the bud."* My kids continue to razz my efforts to make a phone call and now my wife is giving me her infamous stink-eye. I'm sure I'll think of something to appease her, right now I have to...oh no. My battery is dying on my phone! A search for my charger reveals my failure to pack it. *"How is this freakin' possible?"* my mind screams.

The only thing I can do at this point is try to hide violating my promise to unplug from the others. I must nip this office crisis in the bud. I must find a phone charger. If only someone in the family had the same phone I did! I'll wait until the family is busy with a game they are getting organized to go play. No one will notice if I sneak away for a minute. I notice that thought, it feels terrible. It's out of integrity. I feel terrible when I am out of integrity with myself. Shit. It's only the second day of a seven-day trip. I'm in trouble.

"Need to regroup, need to regroup," I repeat out loud. I need a security blanket and this chant feels like one. Calming myself, I can see I need a plan B to stay in integrity and make the necessary calls.

I still recall Karen's howling laughter when I shared this story. "Isn't ego just the best teacher? It wants to stay in integrity and violate the promise!" was her declaration in-between fits of laughter.

I've lost track of all family activity. I've been on the hunt for a phone charger. I've searched every logical place in the family luggage and I'm now looking in drawers and closets of the rental. Stumbling upon the owners office, I think I might have died and gone to office heaven. He's a Mac guy—me too. I'm hopeful I'll find a compatible cord. After a time I look out the office window and notice the bocce ball game had ended. I don't know where everyone has gone. I can't think about that now, I must find a charger.

I've turned my phone off to save battery power and my search has not yielded results. I continue to the basement of the house and I am greeted by every kind of cord and plug known to man. Each is neatly bound and hanging on a pegboard for easy display. Eureka! I've hit the mother lode. Eagerly I begin to search the board for the charger I need.

Wait, how is this possible—every power cord ever made is hanging in front of me—but the one I need!

I need to go to town. Yes, that is my new plan B. Go into town and then I will find the cord I need. Honestly, I don't even remember the excuses I gave the family for the trip into town. I can only recall the relentless push of ego asserting that I must find a way to talk with the office and the sadness in Kath's eyes that I didn't acknowledge.

A few miles down the road I decide to turn my cell phone on. It finds a signal. Yes! Thank you God. Then my phone begins the signaling of messages waiting in my voicemail. Oh dear God. There are eight. *How is that possible? I'm on VACATION!*

I begin to listen to the messages; I can't take it. I terminate the fourth message mid stream. More of the same shit I was promised wasn't going to transpire anymore. What kind of leader tells everyone what they want to hear and then doesn't think they will be upset when they find out smoke was blown up their skirts? I'm most concerned about the upset customer. That impacts revenue. I'll focus on fixing that problem and all else will have to wait until I return. I'm on vacation, after all.

"Greg, it's Jim. I've forgot my phone charger and have very little battery left, give me the cliff notes—what the hell is going on?" Greg's part of the management team and one of the few I totally trust.

Six minutes later my battery dies, leaving me sorry I called. I feel robbed of my vacation. Now all I'm going to do is worry, frustrated that there is nothing I can do about the mess. I'm stuck and depressed. I detest this feeling. I notice that.

"There must be a better way," I tell myself.

Okay, what's the first thing Karen would have me do? In a moment it flashes—*"Clean up"*. I notice my ego squirms at the thought. Clean up is a powerful mixture of loving honesty, amends and realignment with your true self. I've been required on many occasions to do clean up for my weekly homework.

I know from past experience I will feel better and there will be a way to handle this situation that will bring me peace and be truly helpful to everyone, including me. *It's about trust and surrender,* echoes in my mind. In a flash I recall Karen's warning—something about feeling like a two-by-four across my head if I do not practice. Now I know what she meant.

"Growth is not for wimps," I moan to myself as I massage the latest two-by-four blows delivered by…by whom exactly? *Would a loving Universe stick it to me this way?"* my ego ventures.

There is a part of me clawing for control and it wants to know more about the drama. It wants certainty of outcomes (as it defines certainty). I feel some growth, with this insight. *I wonder if this is how a snake feels shedding an old skin?* Separated from the confinement of the old skin, I realize I don't like it. It feels like—like—well, I don't know what it feels like, other than dead-end yuck, going nowhere, more of the same shit yuck.

I'm close to something: I can feel the energy shifting and no sooner than that comes the epiphany, ***"It's me that does this to ME."*** Ego whimpers as it scurries for cover and pretends it doesn't know what I mean. *"So this is the power of the authentic self,"* I oooh and aaaah. *"Wow."* Faced with the power of Spirit, ego disappears. *"Wow."* I wonder if Karen knows this…. I laugh. Duh. Of course she does—it's what she's been saying! **"You have everything you need in this moment to be happy and successful Jim."**

Upon arriving in town I no longer want to search for a power cord.

I surrender. I trust—for the moment anyway. I'm not fooling myself that I can derail the drama train at work; it's happening…what is that prayer?

"God grant me the serenity to accept the things I cannot change,
the courage to change the things I can,
and the wisdom to know the difference."

Wisdom to know what I can change and what I can't?

How many times have I skipped over that meaning? Looking out the car window, the lake catches my eye. Its peaceful surface mocks my turbulent mind.

I feel like a drunk who has been on a bender for days and has just stumbled to the mirror in the bathroom—it's not a pretty site.

Okay, get a grip, I tell myself. *What would Karen have me do?* I know I can always call her...oh yeah. I can't. My phone is dead. I hear, *"Surrender, trust—I have everything I need."*

I'm lifted by the impulse to get my cleanup done. I turn the car around and head back to the mountain house. I don't know what I am going to say; I pray the words will come. I feel foolish, but I also feel lighter and altered. I ask the Universe for it to be for the better.

Entering the long driveway of the mountain house, I happen to glance at the bag of beer sitting on the passenger seat of the car. My pride won't let me confess the real purpose of my sojourn. Letting Kath down has brought me down. I need to recover for me as much as for her. I gave myself one of my trademark pep talks on my return drive. I'm feeling exposed and my monkey-mind has reemerged urging caution: *"Have some good excuses ready,"* it's chanting.

"I promised you I would unplug for the entire week. I didn't keep my promise, I'm sorry. No more office check-ins," I tell Kath.

"Jim, your phone is dead. So you can't. More to the point, when you are with the family—you are not with the family. I knew you couldn't do it anyway, so it's fine. Really." she says, even though I know it's not fine.

"Fair enough. That's true," I respond, fighting a monster urge to be defensive. I want to say, "I 'have to' work—I do it for you and the kids!"

With Karen's admonishment ringing in my ears, *"No excuses, just choices,"* I note growth really isn't for wimps. I release a big sigh and unclench my jaws as I force myself to practice my cleanup.

I begin to walk away and something stops me. I turn back towards Kath and quietly say, "Hey, I'm sorry." We lock eyes. "I'm going to try my best to practice being in the moment. I really want this to be a great vacation—for all of us." We both hear the kids laughing downstairs. "I'm going to join whatever game their playing...if they'll have me." I'm encouraged by her smile. I hope she feels my sincerity. It's true that my endless to-do list often overshadows the expression of love in my heart. Note to self: *One more thing I definitely need to change.*

A new day brings renewal. Kath might think I've snuck out to do office work, but I haven't. I'm watching the brilliant glory of the summer sunrise and it frees my mind from the constant pull to the office crisis dujour.

Have I ever done this? Taken the time to just be? To breathe?

In my good student earnestness, I'm rising early, taking my coffee down to the lake, and journaling. I'm not in the old pattern of making to-do lists; rather, I'm opening to the creative energy Karen is assuring me is present if I plug into it.

Truth be told, I'm half-frustrated. Plugging in sounds so simple yet has been elusive. *Why am I so reactive to the problems at work?* Maybe it's because I am trying to prevent more problems. Opening my notebook, I journal how much I hate the energy drain from the layers of drama draped over the top of each and every problem. *It doesn't have to be this way. We don't need to make everything so hard, so exhausting.*

I feel a surge of anger as I re-play Frank expressing to me that Sam, the CFO, is questioning my value to the company. Under my sales leadership, the company has diversified its portfolio of clients and grown to record highs—both top line revenue and bottom line margin. Despite all this, Frank allows petty jealousies to fester—I suspect he even feeds them. *Why? Can't he see how that impacts the entire company?*

It appears Sam has been jealous of me since my hire. He's a stout man who has a way of drawing attention to how short he is. His eyes are locked in a beady stare from the constant scrutiny of what I do and how I do it. I've dealt with him honestly—I've been respectful of him in deference to his position as CFO. That respect hasn't been a two-way street. I've gotten wind of a new chart he has prepared for the upcoming executive meeting that paints a tainted view of the growth numbers I am so proud of. *Does Frank actually believe the shit Sam is telling him?*

There! I caught it! The trigger for my 'what's happening at the office?' itch.

I don't trust Sam and I suspect the change Frank says he wants is only lip service. It's that simple.

I've been using our growth to introduce a new level of leadership, one that's based upon valuing employees, paying them for the value they provide, as well as mentoring them and holding them accountable for their results. Frank and Sam make it difficult to drive alignment. It's hard to tell what is true and what isn't. I note another source of energy leak.

I'm stunned by the clarity and certainty of this revelation. It resonates in my core. *Is this what being plugged-in feels like?* I can feel my energy lift, as if the Universe has whispered, "yes" in my ear.

As if the lake has just materialized, I wonder why it's tranquility beckons to me. Pondering the lake, a second bolt of clarity hits me: I interact with others under a completely false belief that I can control their choices. When I socialize my message, prepare my message, and deliver it perfectly, my listener will agree with me. That's why I've been desperate to call the office—I want to get my message out. Karen's asked me to notice the way I "sell" my points of view. I'm downright evangelical at times; I've always called it "passionate," but now I can see what she means. My heart sinks as I recall several instances Kath has also tried to point this out to me. *What did I do in response?* The lake, I imagine, is an old friend and has become my confessional. I was defensive when Kath tried to highlight this character flaw. I suppose it was my way of avoiding the truth in what she was saying.

I'm spending so much energy on what others are thinking or doing that I lose all connection to my source of energy and power—me.

I notice the impulse to get out of my dock chair and put my hands in the lake as if it has the power of absolution. I'm humbled by how much I have to let go of, how much I need to change. As successful as I think I am, it doesn't seem possible that I could be so wrong about where my true power lies. I would heartily agree I can't control others—but I don't consistently act in alignment with that truth. The coldness of the water echoes that truth in my mind.

As the week passes I find it easier to disconnect—"unhook" is the word Karen uses, from the details at the office. Unhooking clearly needs to be a major theme for my return to the office. The more I unhook the more clarity I have. Who knew! My monkey-mind activates with the assertion, *how can I not care what is happening?* It appears it will say anything to hook me. Mental memo: *remember that.*

On my sixth day, I wistfully note I have only one more morning by the lake with what is now my early sunrise ritual. Aside from the lake, I've made another new friend, the Universe. In the past few days I've grown close to it, even though it is nameless and faceless. I remember hearing something from the priest in church about a peace that passes all understanding. I never seemed all that peaceful, so I didn't fully understand the peace he was describing. But this new peace, the one I found this week is something I get. I understand it's available to me now and forever. I want to keep the peace in a warm embrace as I would a life-long friend. I silently tell the lake and the surrounding mountains I'm going to take their picture so I will always have a reminder. I suspect I'm going to need a few.

The week's end gives rise to a resolute commitment within to keep the precious peace and clarity I have found as I move out of vacation mode and back to 'real life.' I imagine an astronaut on re-entry to the atmosphere must feel some trepidation at returning to 'reality.' I feel a kinship to the astronaut as I notice I'm dreading my return to the office.

I must make a plan to keep the momentum I've built with the lake, my confessor and new friend, the Universe. I must have the discipline to stay this new course is my mantra. I'm excited about what I have found within me—but I can feel anxiety building around the *'how'* to maintain it.

Making the Shift—
Creating Space for Something Better

I eagerly write my weekly update for my session with Karen. The feeling of an internal shift is a constant state I find myself in. I don't have a name for how or what is happening and I'm fine with that. I'm certain of my steps even though I don't know where I am going. In my update, I carefully, reinforce the magical time with the family in the Adirondacks. It was a new experience to be present with them unlike times past. I'm worried I'll lose what I have found and I want Karen to be clear with me about "how" to maintain the peace and clarity of mind. *What if she doesn't know?* "Christ Jim, don't downshift into doubt," I scold myself. *"Trust, Surrender—the Universe knows how. Have Faith.*

"Jim it's easier than you think—in fact, don't overthink it!" Karen chuckles. She frequently tells me I'm overthinking everything. "You created space with your vacation morning ritual. You gave the Universe your undivided attention and you kept at it—even on the mornings monkey mind was busy retelling a story about this or that. Your experience of connectedness required space for Being, not thinking."

"Creating Space," I repeat. I like—no, I love how that sounds. This is another practice tool I must add to my repertoire. "Unpeel that for me." I respond.

"Do you remember the homework assignment I gave you a while back—to sit in a comfortable place and do nothing other than breathe?"

Boy, did I remember. My first experience was like nails on a chalkboard. Every small sound was amplified; the clock ticking on the wall drove me batty. My mind kept trying to fill the no-space with something. "Oh, yeah I remember," I say.

"You want clarity, you want to get outside your own head," Karen continues. "But filling your head with concerns your ego professes are important keeps you in your head. The problem isn't the monkey in your head, Jim, it's that you believe it when it speaks to you. This is what we all do; it's at the very core of our human experience."

I notice I have been holding my breath. As I force myself to take in air, I'm jittery. "That's deep," I say while pushing out air from my lungs. I'm stuck on the depth and truth of what Karen just said. I believe my opinions. Especially when I am hooked.

"So the answer is to create space—a place where you can observe your own thinking, and then take the skill with you in your day. At first, you'll notice that you got hooked after you got hooked. Then you begin to notice in the moment—then you'll be able to see the triggers as they are coming."

Suddenly I'm frustrated. I can't see how I can apply this to real life. Pushed like a mental volcano, Sam's 'new' accounting gymnastics fill my mind and out of my mouth spills, "Did I tell you what Sam is doing now?" Without waiting for an answer I describe in detail the new spreadsheet he has presented Frank. The spreadsheet contorts logic and the facts so Sam looks like he is making more money for the company than I do as the COO. I'm throwing details at Karen like nails. In the midst of my eruption, I notice I am completely hooked.

"I know this is monkey-mind, I know I'm hooked! But aren't there some things you should be hooked about?" I protest. "How can I create space when the asshole is trying to get me fired?"

As I take a breath, Karen guides me: "You can be right or you can be happy. Choose happy and you are always right."

"I don't know what to do with that," I say, confused.

"Of course there is a part of you that feels like you have to defend yourself—you are human with an ego. But you don't have to react, respond out of that defensiveness." After a long silence Karen adds, "Your safety in the world of form relies upon your defenselessness."

I know what she said is critical, but it's like a puzzle centerpiece—I don't have the edges for it to fit somewhere in my mind.

"Try this," Karen continues, "'Sam, I'm confused about your intention with this chart. What is it that you are trying to say?' Then pay attention to his answer—either he'll come out and say he wonders about your value or he'll retreat from his implication. If he does the former you can state that he is not the CEO and that your value is not within his function to judge as CFO. If it's the latter try: 'so are you saying you want to put numbers together as the CFO that are not relevant to our profit and margin?'"

"Notice how you do not defend yourself in either example. You are simply observing 'what it is' Sam is trying to say, reflecting it back and keeping the conversation focused on the intentions of the chart."

"Can you feel the peace this path would give you, Jim?" Karen finishes.

A puzzle piece clicked in place. "I get it, I'm right with you," I tell Karen.

"Defending is the choice we make when we want to be right. Clarity and saying, 'what it is,' is the choice we make when we want to be happy."

Like so many other golden nuggets I've been gathering in the last few months, I collect this one and write it in my journal.

"The only way to stay unhooked and make the happy choice is if you create space in your mind for another way to see the situation. It's about the chart, it's not about you."

"So you are saying my habit is to defend—I think that's normal," I offer.

Karen laughs, "yes, it's normal—but I thought you didn't want normal."

I join Karen in laughing. "So true, so true."

I've decided I don't need to give up my morning time—just because I am not on vacation. I make a commitment that I will not check email until I have had my quiet time to journal and plug in to my spiritual self. It may only be twenty minutes, it may be an hour, but absolutely no skipping this devotion to my growth. Part of my weekly homework includes reporting how well I did with this. I'm going for seven out of seven days each week.

I notice I have energy when I get up in the morning, an hour earlier than normal. I'm excited about the increased voltage I feel running through me. At the same time I'm calmer than I have ever been. Charged and calm! The polarity strikes me.

My weeks meander like a stream getting closer and closer to the river. I feel slow and steady learning, growing, and repeating the process. Most of my attention and energy is being directed toward removing the clutter. “Even if you add good to the crap pile, eventually it becomes crap.” That’s how Karen describes clutter’s toxic energy. It contaminates everything. “Look at the world, Jim. Can you find one toxic item that has not infiltrated and poisoned everything it touches?”

From the moment Karen uses the phrase: “Remove the clutter,” I am enchanted. Cleaning out the basement and closets of my mind, it is a constant discovery of beliefs and thoughts that had been locked away.

“The only way to get something better is to remove the clutter. Sometimes the clutter is what the world would call ‘good’,” Karen adds. “The only way you’ll know is if you keep careful track of your energy leaks. Energy leaks are terrific pointers to the clutter that needs to be removed.” Henceforth one of my primary on-going homework assignments is to keep a list of my energy leaks. When I first began the assignment it was directed only at work. I sense this is about to change.

Speak to the Heart of the Matter

I had resisted spending any of my session time with Karen on my mother, sisters, or the declining situation my father was in due to his health and live in girlfriend. I had not spoken to my older sister in years, and visiting time with my mother was kept to a minimum. My mantra was, "They will never change, so why bother?" During my journaling one day I could see it wasn't about them changing. The same tool I had been using at work, with greater and greater success, I now knew I need to use on my birth family.

At work, the Sam situation unfolded with ease and grace for me. Without any prompting on my part, Frank decided to change Sam's role. Everyone sensed he was being phased out of the company, mostly by his choices: his past posturing and deception over who offered more value led others to really see him for who he was. He didn't change one bit, neither did anyone else, but I certainly did. Even though he was CFO, part of the value he asserted for himself was as a sales person who had key contacts at targeted accounts. So Frank put him to his word and made him a sales guy—who now reported to me.

My list of energy leaks was like lifting a drape covering priceless art. It revealed a lasting treasure. Every arrow Sam shot at me I absorbed with greater and greater ease. I kept my focus on "Being who I wanted to be—authentic, engaged, and inspiring." To me that meant being helpful, supportive and focused on where we were going as a company and the road maps needed to get there.

What company would I ever work at or with where I would never meet difficult individuals? There was an endless supply of them, yet my change meant I would never be at a loss for my peace of mind. I was the master of my energy, my power, and my life. God, this felt good.

"I can feel it coming," I told Karen one session. "I need to find a way to deal with my mother and my sisters. I know my practice at work needs to extend into other areas of my life."

"Good for you, Jim. Crap is crap—and these buckets we tend to divide our lives into always find a way to seep into the other parts of our life. There's no point cleaning up the clutter in one area and not generalizing it to all areas."

Karen had me do an exercise I found intriguing. I made a dot in the middle of a page; then I drew three uniform circles around the dot leaving about two inches between each circle. I was the dot. I was to fill the spaces between the circles with the people in my life. My inner circle was to be those closest to me—regardless of my biological relationship to them. In the second circle was the next group, who I didn't feel were in the first, but I felt close to and made efforts to extend and continue friendships. Then the final circle was everyone else who came to mind.

My mother was in my last circle. Except for a few, the same was true for everyone at the office. It spoke volumes to me about the power I gave others in my life. Power they didn't ask for—yet I surrendered. This was not the kind of surrender I wanted to be practicing!

Despite the numerous declarations I made about how impossible my mother was to have a conversation with and the extensive examples of her negativity about the past, her divorce from my father, and life in general I provided, Karen was unyielding. "Jim, the point of a Universal truth is that it is always true." Karen added, "Try this: 'Mom, I'd love to have regular pleasant conversations with you. I know you are upset about life, but when you keep beating the past like a dead racehorse you expect will still get up and win the race—the conversation is not uplifting.'"

"Dead-on again," I tell Karen.

"Say what it is, Jim!"

"What if she won't listen?"

"Jim, she doesn't have to listen. You just have to affirm your desire for a positive relationship, and when it isn't, say: 'Mom, this is a good example of what I am talking about—I won't listen to this, so I am going to hang up now. I hope we can talk later when you feel more positive.

"Make the space for something better, Jim. Get rid of the clutter."

Karen suggested that I write my mom a letter—one from my heart. I felt this was my better option. I could write in the morning—connected and plugged in. Sending the letter off, I knew she may not change and indeed may not receive my letter well—but I was choosing happy. Moreover, I was inviting her to join me in that choice. I scheduled a trip to visit her, to share my thoughts and practice saying 'what is.' The clarity of my intentions ushered in a newfound peace.

In quiet time, I began journaling about 'speaking from the heart.' *What a bum rap that has been given in our world—especially the business world!* Our charts, goals and to-do lists suggest heart has nothing to do with our success. *What else matters besides heart?* I've coached my son's AAU basketball team for years; I look first and foremost for the heart in each player. Our team achieves far more success with heart than talent.

"What exactly is success, Jim?" Karen inquired.

"Well, um, well...." We both started laughing. "Let me guess," I said. "Put that on my homework list?"

"Yes, but don't force it. Let it reveal itself to you. Note your list of energy leaks; they will inform you what it isn't. Authentic success is different for each person. It's based upon the Authentic you—the real you."

In coaching basketball, success could easily be defined as a win. Winning a game, a season, a title—most people use winning to judge success in sports. My experience—the experience of my heart—was very different. As a coach, I struggled to balance the wins on the court with the personal win each player achieves from many life lessons he learns. Perseverance, discipline, teamwork, commitment, focus—lessons that last a lifetime. Sports can be a wonderful avenue for life lessons. I thought of my role as head coach as sacred. Yes, in my role as coach I was to inspire the players—but I also am a teacher, mentor and guide. Coaching youth sports is the best on-the-job leadership training any executive could ask for.

What was it I was teaching them, exactly?

"We teach what we are learning," Karen told me. "What is it you think you are learning now?"

"There are no short cuts. No magic pills, no secret formulas, and no ten steps. There is simply the ever-present power of the Authentic self and our focus upon where our power truly lies. It's also about a daily moment to moment discipline to connect to that power within."

Encouraging me to continue, Karen asked, "And what do you need to do to find that power?"

"Clarity. Peace of mind. Awareness. Unhook. Speak to the heart of the matter…I know there is more."

"Very good, grasshopper! Of course there is more; there is always more. We never arrive. Success is not a place we get to—it's a state of Being we live in. Your definition of success will evolve as you evolve. Two years from now it will be very different than it is today."

I reminisced over the next few months about each of the goals and milestones I believed when attained would crown my success. Some accomplishments had temporary success. Others were like tarnished silver even before their attainment.

At work I continued to watch the number of self-created urgencies. During our executive board meeting, I noted it was touted that if we solved whatever the problem was in front of us NOW, we'd be successful. Yet, every success metric highlighted in a monthly executive meeting was met with an equal concern that it was either going to get worse or it could all change tomorrow. Two concepts tethered to one another—both destructive ways to view how to grow a company. To complicate matters; in Frank's mind, only a few people carried their weight. He was never satisfied and didn't believe his management team should be either. Greg leaned over and whispered to me, "Why do I feel like I suck—and no matter how much effort I expend we are never successful?" Was it Frank's intent or his delivery that was the problem? Or was it something different?

Greg's question flipped a switch in my mind. I realized the boys' basketball team I coach won more than they lost. We always made it to the championship rounds in tournaments. At the end of each season I took the time to write a personal note to each player highlighting their growth—their success and what I encouraged them to work on in the offseason. Never had I mentioned how many points they scored, as that could never be a measure of their success.

Maybe that is one component of success—always growing and learning? It's not only about the score. Maybe this is why I get frustrated at work—I don't see the other members of the leadership team growing and learning—or wanting to grow and learn.

My mind drifts to family matters, I somehow allowed myself to get triangulated with my dad's girlfriend, my sister's suspicions of her and the growing unrest in our family over my dad's health. *Really, Jim—look how your mind skips around!* I find myself mumbling to myself. "I didn't catch that, Jim," Frank says. I had lost track of the meeting. Surely a sign of a successful meeting would be attentive attendees.

What was I thinking about? Oh, I know: I'm pissed I walked into this pile of drama masquerading as an executive board meeting. I don't answer Frank; I just shake my head.

My faith tells us to do unto others, as you would have them do unto you.

Regardless, I've been watching attacks and counter attacks from all sides over my dad's care—none of it kind. God only knows what lessons our kids are learning. It feels toxic and hypocritical.

No, that's not what I was reflecting on! Talk about toxic clutter infiltrating my mind! *I was mulling success. What is Success?*

One particular goal I set for myself was to write a book about my journey. Everything I learn that I apply to the business world transforms my experience. *I have things of this world, great things—but that doesn't mean I'm happy or successful. When do I feel successful?*

The meeting adjourns with flaming hoops to jump through, I am certain none of which will lead to success. I think everyone else knows that too. I put this on my review list with Karen. Something has to change, I know it's me—but I don't know the how or what. I don't feel as successful as I want to, that's for sure.

During my drive home from the meeting, I can't let go of the question: *What is success? What would be success with my dad's situation?* "Showing up differently," floats into my mind. When I'm practicing, using the tools I've learned, having a different experience of my experience, I am as light as a cloud.

How does this apply to the drama around my dad's girlfriend?

My journaling about the mess leads me back to the basics: **Say what it is.** I want our family to practice the values we say we have. I can't support this bickering. The main instigators keep pecking at me. *What's my take on the situation?* I wonder.

Looking in the mirror, I have to fess up. I took the bait. Gave my opinion. Stupid. "Opinions are not facts!" Karen stresses over and over. "When in doubt, say your intention." I didn't do that very well.

My spine straightens as I commit: *Say what it is, from the heart. Say what I desire. Unhook; let it be.* That may be easier said than done. My opinion was contorted. I've been accused of saying and doing things I have not. A very vocal part of me wants everyone to know, "It's not true! I didn't say that!"

"Handle this the same way you did your mom and Sam, Jim" Karen encourages. "You are not in charge of other people's lessons and learning. Moreover, judging others because you don't think they are learning will cause suffering—mostly for you. You don't have to agree with them and only your ego mind would tell you that unhooking might make it look like you agree with what they are doing."

I make a visit to see my dad and talk to both him and his girlfriend. I want to be clear about my position and express my concern for my dad, in front of both of them. Then let it go. I decide to end any in-depth conversations with his fracturing girlfriend—smile, say hi, but not get hooked when I see her. Karen's line, "Everyone has a right to be wrong," helped me 'let it be.' The visit could have been a disaster. The visit is stormy, but in the midst of storm, I am at peace. *Who'da thunk?* I smile to myself as I review the visit in my mind on the drive home.

Making room for something better by removing the clutter and pinning down success have been carrying me through my second year of active practice. One nagging piece of making room and clearing the clutter is the constant cycle of clutter at work. Every process and procedure I have put in place has had positive results. Lately, I feel like I'm pushing Jell-O up a mountain. No matter how far I get it up the mountainside, some slips around me and falls down the mountain. It's the proverbial back to square one, over and over again.

Old Me...New Me

I start my next session with Karen by declaring that I need to go out on my own—again. I'm not meant to work forever in a company. Especially when the leadership changes its mind like a winter wind about what is important today. The last executive board meeting put me over the edge. I can't feel successful in this environment. It's clear Frank doesn't want to change. It's his company, he doesn't have to—but change is what he has hired me for. It's a clear conflict. I'm sure he's thinking of how to phase me out like he did Sam. He's torn though; I can see it. He sees my value. No one can replace me; we both know it!

In our session Karen and I cover the "either/or" ego thinking and the "both/and" thinking of Spirit. Both/and is elusive to me. How can I take the necessary steps to go out on my own and come up with a plan for the company's success? It doesn't make sense.

"You are torturing yourself with the cursed 'how's' again, Jim! What is your job?" Karen asks.

"Show up fully, do everything I can with what I have from where I am." I answer.

We came up with action items based upon those authentic criteria for action.

Greg and I spent several working sessions fleshing out Frank's stated vision of becoming chairman of the board and having me become President and Greg the COO. We both agree there needs to be many changes if we want to have sustainable growth and position the company for a profitable sale. I've been watching Frank thrash against the new vision. The same vision he announced and says he wants. Why is it we can always see clearly in others what they can't see in themselves?

Frank has begun dangling the potential sale of the company in front of me. I think he should accept an offer, if it's really true, and I tell him so. I know he won't, regardless of the price offered. His identity is tied up in the company. Like so many others, Frank thinks he is what he does for income. His identity is the company. He'll hang on to it. The only real question in my mind is how I'll exit the company, sale or no sale.

My monkey-mind begins to jump around in the trees.

No, 'how I exit' is not the only question! What's my offering to my clients? How will I package it? Where is my plan? Like the gathering winds of a thunderstorm my monkey-mind begins to churn. I need to begin to make plans, take steps—a change is coming, I can feel it.

"Holy crap!" Karen says at our next session as I lay out my "to-do" list. "Look at you all twisted up." I can hear the smile in her voice. Laughing at yourself is one of the great lessons in my sessions with Karen. She reminds me how hard I am on me. I need to soften, be compassionate towards myself. I hear "be a slacker" most of the time when she tells me this—no, that's not true—my ego mind says "slacker." I smile at the awareness. I notice the path I need to go down to expand my power, is exactly what the monkey-mind will beat me up about.

"Having a different experience of your experience is the point of a Spiritual Practice," Karen reminds me. "The old you would man the battle stations, frantically make lists, have action items, and assign dates to have them done by..."

The monkey-mind volcano erupts. I've learned over the course of our sessions to smile at it—acknowledge its presence—but don't get hooked by it. Just listen and then be honest about what it is objecting to. "So here's what my monkey-mind is saying," I tell Karen. "If we don't make lists and assign completion dates, we will never achieve our goals. Goals are a good thing!"

"So what does the Authentic you have to say, Jim?"

I marvel at what a good question that is. I've never asked that question before.

"So you know what the old you would say. What does the NEW you say?" As soon as Karen finishes the question I know the answer:

"There is a better way."

Quickly I tag-it, *I know this is monkey-mind—again—but it's screaming 'how?' Knowing there is a better way—and knowing the how of the better way—those are two different things.*

"Very true. What if you are only in charge of one of those things, Jim?"

"What?"

"Divine Intelligence, The Universe, God—whatever name you want to use is in charge of the how. You have help; you only have to be a good receiver of the help. When you think it's your job to do it all by yourself—you are closed to the help."

Even my ego-monkey has stopped swinging in the branches of my mind. I notice the deep sigh of relief that comes from 'I am not in charge of the how'; my Spirit tells me this is what I am learning to Surrender to.

Then the inspired thought comes, *"It's like I tell my AAU players,"* I venture, "Let the game come to you?"

"Exactly!"

"I have to be honest, I resonate with everything you just said, Karen, but I can feel my monkey-mind trying to argue. I tell my players to play the ball, move with the ball, the mastery is over one's self—not the other team."

"So I'll remind you: you do not fight with your own mind. Remember the mantra I gave you for your monkey-mind: 'Thank you for sharing.' This is how you create space from it. Give the new you a moment to enter—it will."

"I like that. Old me...New me. I feel clear when I can identify a specific behavior as the old me or new me," I say.

"That's how you know you are on your path and not someone else's."

"I do feel like I should be doing something about work," I admit.

"Let's reaffirm our Trust," Karen encourages. "Yes, undoubtedly you will have action items. The new you needs to ask what they are—before the old you decides what they are. Most of the time we make up our mind what we want to do—then we ask the Universe to bless it. We have our order completely mixed up!" she laughs. "Don't you think that if you have a job to do the Universe would tell you what it is?"

I understand exactly what Karen is saying. The folly of a belief that the Universe would give us a job to do and keep it a secret makes me smile too.

"Your job is to create the space—and listen. You'll get pointers and help from your daily life," Karen reminds me.

I'm buoyed—completely grateful for yet another profound shift I am feeling. As we end our session I take the floating feeling into the day.

As the next few weeks unfold, I meet individuals who made requests of me to share with their companies some of my mini-workshops. I present my workshop "ME INC." in various formats. It is always very well received. Karen points out how invigorated I am by the experience and gives me a homework assignment to invite more workshop experiences into my life. *Maybe this is something that should go on my offering list?*

I smile as I notice the monkey-mind eagerly awaiting permission to take off making a list. *The new me,* I remind myself *will keep the space and ask the Universe if this is something I should be considering.*

More and more my creative energy is flowing. The more I practice; the ideas and answers stream effortlessly. I notice the improvement in the quality of the idea itself. Sure, I always had good ideas. But these ideas are great. I'd like for the creative flow to be like a garden hose—full blast when I want it to be and stored when I'm not using it. I notice that thought feels like my ego monkey. "So it must be," Karen would say to me.

Ooh. How cool is that! Lately, I've been able to know what Karen would say with regularity. I make a note to proudly report these instances to Karen, confident she'll celebrate with me. *Of course she would correct me slightly—she is just telling me how the Universe works.* "It's like repeating a message, it's not *'my'* special message" Karen has a melody in her voice when she tells me this. I know she's sung this song to many others.

I've mentioned to my network on a handful of occasions that I'm beginning to do mini-workshops to help re-direct and focus the energy of employees. Each time I mention the workshop; it receives a welcome and quickly finds a home. While I enjoy this, I feel as if I'm going in way too many directions. I want to get my book done; I want to write more. Each time I prepare and create a workshop, it's time I don't have for writing.

"Seriously, Jim?" Karen chides me as I tell her this. "You think you live in a Divine Universe that doesn't know how to use all things for good?"

"Ouch. I deserved that." I say. "So what am I missing?"

"Both-AND"

"Huuuuhhh?"

"Ego mind thinks in either-or paradigms: it tells you either you can be writing the book, or you can be preparing for a workshop." She lets that sink in.

"It's Both-AND. Don't you think, that a divine, all-knowing source energy would be able to do that?"

"You mean material for my workshops should go in my book?" As soon as I say it I begin to chuckle at my old self foolishness.

"Ding! Ding! Ding!" Karen says joining my chuckles.

Like a lightening flash the book content is illuminated. I want to discuss it further until Karen says, "So how's your wife?"

The bright book flash is gone as quick as it came.

I've been mentioning over the last few months that Kath is struggling—or so it seems to me—with some of the day-to-day changes life throws at us. Karen has been great at educating me about what women face in a world so focused on being a young, skinny supermodel. "Just like you are learning to honor yourself, Jim, so is Kathy. You are different people, so you will do it in different ways. But that doesn't mean you can't honor each other and do it together."

Kath has been my true love since college. There was something special about her, about us, from the day we met. Like a pair of matching gloves, we fit together perfectly. Today, we are friends, lovers, supporters, and cheerleaders to each other. I definitely know I am changing and sense she is too. Karen has made me mindful the ego-monkey thinks that change is its playground. I'm learning to be supportive without rescuing. "Try shutting up, Jim!" Karen says. "Listen with your heart to her—not the ego mind that says you need to have the answer for her. Let her know you are sorry this is a tough time, but you are here for her—then be there."

"I do that," I tell Karen. "Well, at least I think I do that." As soon as I say it, I regret it.

"You mean you don't try to talk her out of feeling the way she does?" Karen inquires.

I've learned there is no point in offering excuses. I don't have anything I want to defend, just mindsets I want to clear out of my head. Thank you God, for my practice.

Karen continues, "I want you to take a breath, and listen to my question—with as open a mind as the new you can possibly muster. I don't want you to answer me. I want you to sit with how uncomfortable you are with the question."

"Let me get my seat-belt on." I answer.

"Is it possible what you are trying to do with Kathy is 'fix her' so that you can be left alone—without guilt—to pursue the new ventures coming your way?"

Oh crap! Ego mind is running around like a bronco let out of the shoot. It's been exposed. *I do not want to admit I do this, but I don't know how to object to the truth.*

"I'll have to think about that one," I say dismissively. "It's probably a guy thing," I mumble. As my words trail off, I realize that is just some excuse I convince myself is true. *It has nothing to do with being a 'guy.' How lame am I to even try to blame it on that?*

Karen doesn't notice she's been dismissed. "The old you did this so you could pursue work—and work is a damn good cover for why you are not available. Have the homework assignments I've given you been effective?"

Karen has me pinned down and she's not going to let me go. Truth is I don't want her to. It's just my stupid ego man-pride at work. Even I know that.

"Yes, it's made a big difference," I report. It's not that my relationship with Kath has ever been bad. But we've become robots doing what we've always done, just trying to get through this week, this month. I am deathly afraid that I will wake up one morning and find out after a life of love and three wonderful kids we grew apart. As a child, I lived through three divorces and witnessed first hand the slippery slope many married people face trying to manage it all. While I love my dad dearly, he took the easy way out on multiple occasions. Externally, I beam with pride when everyone says we are so much alike. Internally, my antenna is overly sensitive to even the most remote potential warning signals when it comes to marriage.

Some time ago, when I first hinted at this concern, Karen eased my mind, "Jim, this is one of the hardest things for all of us when we are evolving. We are afraid we will leave the other behind. We get stuck between the old us and the new us out of fear."

I scheduled time to walk with Kath. It's something we both like to do. In the midst of our very busy schedules we often don't have much time together.

I reported to Karen the improbability that something so simple could be so effective. Of course we weren't just walking, we were talking—and I was practicing being present, attentive and affirming the ways I cherished Kath.

My wondering mind comes back to our session when Karen says bluntly, "Jim, you are trying to manage Kathy for your benefit."

I don't miss a beat as I declare, "I want to change that—now."

The synchronicity of the Universe is a beautiful thing. My anniversary was coming up soon. Karen observed the ways I honored my role as a dad with my kids on their sixteenth birthdays: I wrote them each a letter. When they graduated high school, I gave them a personalized version of a book I wrote just for my kids, called the "Keys to Success," sprinkled with appreciation and wisdom. The kids often tease me for speaking in metaphors—they tell me it's cheesy. The book unpacks my favorite sayings to them—much to my surprise, both girls loved it and treasured the book. I look forward to doing the same for my son when he graduates.

"Why don't you find a similar way to lavish Kathy with the appreciation you have for her?"

"What a great idea! I can make a book for her—a journal on all the things I appreciate her doing—for me, for our family." Ideas explode in my head like fireworks on the fourth of July. Without notice, my mind shifts to "my" book. Like a train approaching the station, the brakes in my head are screeching. *When am I going to find the time?* Before I even mention it, Karen offers, "Both-AND Jim. It's your new mantra, no more either-or." She is reading my mind—again.

Ego vs. Spirit

My annual review with Karen is approaching and I want to present an update on my book. I've been using my journal, my notes, and my lists and writing my fingers numb. *Would I feel successful if I actually finished the book? Ahh, Success. What are you? Yes, I think I would consider it one of my better successes to finish the book.*

As Karen and I discuss our upcoming annual review, I declare, "I'm ready to show you what I have written so far." I make excuses about it not being finished and know that it still needs tweaking—but I want to dedicate part of our work together on getting the book done. I feel I have made substantial progress on this goal by writing what I have thus far.

"We need to talk about power vs. force, Jim." Karen's tone perks me up. I know something important is coming. "You are at the middle of your story, Jim. I can't tell you what is coming for you, but knowing the Universe, it's great. And it'll continue your lessons. That means you have more material for the book. You are not done."

I'm a bit sullen. Karen adds, "Yes, you can have a goal. Yes, the goal can be to write a book." Karen pauses. "The question is do you want it to be just a book? Or would you like for it to be a piece of you—from your heart? You know, Authentic?"

There it is again! I remind myself. *Rushing to the end, hurrying to finish the goal, forgetting the journey! Argh.* Getting so focused on the goal and forsaking the 'why' of the goal has been a component of my discontent.

"Yeah, yeah—you caught me." I chuckle. "No more empty goals. No more goals simply for the sake of putting a check mark next to something I accomplished so I could falsely congratulate my ego."

"Tell me, what makes your heart sing, Jim?"

I have to get quiet, and connect within. Instinctively I breathe, the air passing through my lungs opens my mind—the flood of cool, enjoyable parts of my day stream in.

After reciting the joys to Karen, she concludes, "So would you say your enjoyment comes from teaching others how to look at their circumstance in a way that gets better results for everyone?"

"Totally," I conclude.

"So let's look at your book through that filter when we get together next week," Karen offers.

* * * *

I'm excited to show Karen my book draft. I glance at it and smile as I put it in my backpack. I've emailed a version to her, but printing it out—binding it—my pride swells as I imagine her comments.

"I've had a couple of days to read the draft," Karen tells me. I hand her the bound draft copy and she smiles, "Of course you would!" She suggests we start our annual review with the book and I am excited, feeling like I am on my way with the goal of getting it done.

"What are you afraid of?" Karen asks. I'm stunned. I don't know what she is referring to. "It's not that the draft is terrible, Jim. It's just not you." Now I'm really confused.

"It's nothing BUT me!" I exclaim.

"The Jim I know has one of the biggest hearts a Soul can muster. You are open. You share of yourself and from your heart."

"Okay, I'm with you there," I comment.

"This is sanitized. It's not REAL."

I can feel myself shift back and forth in my chair looking for some comfort from the sting of her comment—and then it hits me: *Oh. Dear, God. She's right. I know she's right.*

"Something very cool just happened!" I exclaimed. "Part of me wanted to leap out of my chair and scream, 'How can you say that? But then something even stronger in me knew IT WAS TRUE. And I'm one hundred percent at peace."

"Very, very good! Woo-hoo!" Karen cheers for me.

"Give me some examples," I implore her. "With all my heart, I want the book to be me, to be REAL. Honestly though, I struggle sometimes getting everything out on paper."

"Jim, your story can help so many people. Don't you think that others have the experience of a partnership with another person or company and realize it's not working?"

"Of course, I wrote about that."

"No, Jim, you didn't." Once again, I feel the brick against my head. "You mentioned that you had this company, then it was time to do something else. That's basically what you wrote. You left out the agony of trying to get it to "work." You left out the sleepless nights and frustration of knowing it was not working, the paralyzed fear you had of how to end it. You are not honest about your personal opinions or the internal beliefs you had about the problems the company had."

"Like what?" I counter.

"Like you were doing all of the leg-work and Kevin couldn't move a chess piece. Like you completely regretted going 50-50 with him in the company instead of 51-49."

"I can't be...." I'm struggling for the word and Karen fill's in, "Truthful?"

I catch myself holding my breath. "Why do I have such a hard time saying, 'What is?'" I ask Karen.

"What are you afraid of?" she asks again.

She has a twinkle in her eye. I tell her, "You know those times when I tell you how grateful I am for our time together? This isn't one of them!"

The twinkle gets brighter as she says, "I have all day."

"I don't want to upset anyone," I sigh. "I just want to be cool."

"Massive energy leak. Don't you think there is a way to say 'what is' without judgment? It's judgment and condemnation that's the problem."

A light bulb goes off in my head. I think I may understand something when Karen continues, "The truth is we all have judgment and condemnation—until we learn a better way. The truth is you don't want to own up to this and are sanitizing everything so you don't have to own the judgments you do have."

"Ouch. Double and triple ouch."

"Is it true?" Karen says softly.

"I like you even less right now."

"You are big enough to let this ego trait go. Your Spirit is big enough to handle being human and this will not have any power over you anymore. The question is do you want to be that big?"

A wave of relief comes over me. I realize I have been at the mercy of this shame my entire life. I excel at being cool on the outside. Inside, it's different. Most would be surprised at the competing stories that continuously play in the back of my mind. *I guess that's true for all of us—we hide our dark places.*

"There isn't a person who has ever lived that isn't challenged by the same thing, Jim. Isn't it interesting how our ego minds trick us into thinking we are special and we are the only ones who have this trouble—therefore we need to be ashamed of it?"

"I can't be the only one, of course everyone does it. But I'm not proud of it."

"And that is what makes your life work so much better now, Jim. You spot the energy leak of judgment and you want to change it. I bet you already have some homework in mind to get in front of this," Karen smiles.

"I'll start with a list. I'm good at those," I chuckle. "My daily journaling will now include a list of judgments I've made in the last twenty-four hours. For me, this works. The one thing I am learning is that the more I raise my awareness to the behaviors I want to change, the easier it becomes for me to change them."

"Excellent," Karen agrees.

Karen and I discuss some examples of saying 'what is,' while still being compassionate. I feel like I'm getting the hang of it and I take on re-writes as my long-term homework assignment. "I want to get the book published this year," I mention as part of my re-write commitment.

"Maybe that will happen Jim," Karen says in her serious tone. "And maybe it won't. Power vs. Force."

"Little grasshopper realizes you have mentioned Power vs. Force many times. What am I missing?"

Karen looks at me intently for a moment. I swear I can feel the breath she takes. "How's your dad?" she asks.

"It's interesting you ask," I respond. Karen doesn't shift her gaze, so I continue. "Not good. In fact I'm heading up to Albany this weekend." Then I realize, she knows something, in that way she has. Once when I inquired, "How do you know the things you do?" Karen responded, "The Universe has a language, I have learned to read it and speak it." I'm attracted to the idea of a language—dependable communication I know one day I will decipher.

"You need to practice. We have great power when we accept the things we cannot change. You know your dad doesn't have a great deal of time. Accept that and you will be able to be there for him—and be at peace with the choices he has made that you don't agree with."

"But how will I know what I can't change?"

"Don't force things. Let them unfold. You will know."

The Discipline to Practice

As Kath comes down the path to the beach from the hotel room it registers with me how we have fallen in love all over again. I finally get the concept of authentic intimacy. Over this last year, all that has happened with my dad and his death, Kath's best friend, JoAnn's death, and then our dog Riley's—I guess it was sink or swim for us.

Kath waves to me, pointing to the hotel beach bar; she wants to know if I want a drink. I smile and wave "no." When Kath joins me, she can tell I am lost in thought and have been for some time. At times this used to upset her; today she gently asks if I want more quiet time.

"No," I respond, "I was just thinking about everything that has happened over the last year. Especially the issues with Pops, Mary—God, that would have been enough to unhinge anyone." I smile and continue, "I'm extremely grateful and take a lot of pride in having the discipline to practice when it counted—the payoff has been huge, not only for my own peace of mind, but for our relationship in particular. I am feeling very blessed right now."

"Are you sure you don't want a drink?" Kath's look over the top of her sunglasses says it all.

"You know, maybe I will. Get me the one I had yesterday—what's it called, the Rum Runner? Yeah, I think that's it."

As Kath gets the drinks from the beach bar, I debate if I want to continue the conversation. I'm not sure I'm in the mood to rehash the events of the last year, when it occurs to me I may not have really told Kath everything.

Sometimes you need a purge, I'm remind myself. *Ah, thank you Universe,* I silently praise my guidance.

Kath hands me my drink and smiles, "One Rum Runner on the rocks."

"It occurs to me," I say as I turn to face her, "I may have not really told you everything. I mean yes, the big picture details, like Mary was stealing from my dad. But did I tell you about Pops' last breaths when I was at his bedside in the hospital?"

"No, you didn't," Kath responds. "Do you want to talk about it now?"

I send the Universe another silent thanks. There was a time when Kath would have misunderstood my omitting information and been hurt or upset.

"You know the visit I made to Albany to see Pops before his series of hospitalizations?" I ask.

"I remember, it was right after you had the book review with Karen."

"Yeah, it was. Anyway, I tape recorded Pops telling me what he wanted to have happen with Mary, the house, all the stuff in the house." I begin to recall telling Pops my discomfort at the situation: *my sisters are convinced Mary was stealing from him, Pops not dealing with Mary in a clear fashion.* "I just wanted to ensure I did things right, honored his wishes. The memory, my memory is a tricky thing. Taping felt appropriate."

"Go on," Kath urges.

"It's hard for me to say this, but he didn't love Mary. I know he had problems with women, just look at his track record. I'm still not sure if he loved his second wife Jean. I never got a sense that he loved my mom—at least not that I knew of." I said. "I definitely knew he loved Marian—it's a shame they never got married. He wanted to, he told me. Mary, on the other hand, was a relationship of convenience. Pops was terrified of being alone. I think he also wanted a helper—a nurse. I guess it's no surprise Mary was a nurse."

"What are you saying?"

"He was really cold about how to take care of her at his death. I mean he was giving her a car he had owned for ten years and thirty days to leave the house she lived in for sixteen years." I tell Kath. "To be fair to Pops, I guess he felt he had been taking care of Mary for the last sixteen years. Mary only worked a few hours a week and didn't contribute to the household expenses. So maybe he thought that was all he felt obliged to give her. In any case, Mary must have known at some level how Pops felt."

"Okay, so?"

"Besides taping our conversation, we completed a total power of attorney for me. I had them notarized at his bank; he gave copies to his attorney. After the call from my sister that Pops was back in the hospital again—and I needed to come quick—I brought a copy of the power of attorney with me. I'm not sure what made me do that, but I remember going back into the house to grab it after we said good-bye in the driveway." I could tell by the look on Kath's face she recalled this kiss good-bye. "I figured I didn't know what condition I'd find Pops in, but since he'd been in and out of the hospital for over six months and several times the last two months, he might need help just getting the bills caught up or sorted out. I planned to do that while I sat by his bedside waiting for the doctor."

"That sounds like you," Kath smiles. "Always the multi-tasker."

"I'm working on it," I confess.

I take a sip of my Rum Runner and notice the clear blue ocean waves pounding the shore. My memory flashes to that day as I used every muscle in my body to fight back the tears. I can tell Kath notices, but I try not to look at her.

"Pops was doing very poorly when I arrived. Val clearly didn't want me driving upset, so she tempered his condition on the phone. When I arrived she gave me the bad news: he was on life support." I ignore the tear running down my cheek and continue, "Val and I were waiting for the doctor. We knew it was decision day. We wondered if Pops could survive without life support or if he would need 24/7 care. Val didn't think he would be able to talk and worried if someone needed to feed him. I remember my mind racing all over the place. The nurse finally came in and said the doctor was going to be delayed a few hours. I almost went crazy. I couldn't sit there. I had to do something. All I kept telling myself was to THINK. What would Pops want me to do? Putting the power of attorney in place seemed like a good place to start. I realized some time had gone by since Pops and I had it notarized and couldn't remember if the bank had kept a copy, so I decided to head to the bank."

I paused a moment as I remember thanking the Universe for the tap on the shoulder to bring the power of attorney with me.

"Somehow things felt urgent. I'm not sure why, but I remember racing to the stairs of the hospital, knowing they'd be faster than the elevator. There was a man in front of me who was moving slow, real slow. He was a large black man, about 6' 6' or more, who looked a lot like Bill Russell, the basketball star from the Boston Celtics. It was no use trying to get around him as I could tell he was not in any hurry. Just as I was about to make my move and pass him at the bottom of the steps, he turned and said "Hello."

"Now, this was not any ordinary "hello." He had that deep penetrating voice like James Earl Jones. I returned the hello and again was about to kick it into high gear and move past him, when he asked me, "Why are you here young man?" 'Seriously?' I remember thinking, my annoyance was high and I hated the feeling. I felt guided to take one breath and then another. Before I realized it, I was walking side by side with him, a complete stranger, spilling my guts about my dad.

"As my worries spilled from my mouth, I said I didn't think my dad was going home. He proceeded to tell me a story about a similar experience he had with his dad and all the different family members and things he had to manage. I was mesmerized by the similarities. All I kept thinking was, "Who is this dude? Where did he come from?" He then looked deeply into my eyes, and told me in that profound voice of his, "Slow down, and take a deep breath. You are stronger than you think." I couldn't move or speak. I just stood there, starring at him. He interrupted the silence by extending his hand and said, "Take care young man." As I walked away, I heard his voice pierce through the muted hospital crowd. "Jim, where are you parked?" I turned and he was waving and walking towards me. "Parking garage," I said. "Here, take this, it's a parking pass – just give it to the attendant and your parking is free for as long as you are here." I grabbed the door handle of my car when it hit me—I don't think I told him my name."

Kath grabs her drink.

"When I got to the bank, I didn't have any trouble putting the power of attorney in place. As the bank manager made a copy of the power of attorney document, I gave my dad's monthly statement a quick look. I stopped dead in my tracks when I noticed two extremely large checks had cleared his account in the last two weeks."

"So what were they for?" Kath asks.

"I didn't know, so I went over to the bank manager's desk and asked him to tell me what the checks were for. I mean, Pops didn't have those kind of bills."

"True, he was very conservative," Kath adds.

"Both were to Mary. The kicker is the bank verified it wasn't Pops' signature on the checks."

"I was wondering how the money was taken." Kath says quietly. "But I never wanted to ask."

"You should have asked!" I say, surprised.

"How could I, Jim? You had so much on your plate. I didn't want to burden you with more stuff to think about. Besides, I knew you'd tell me sooner or later."

I say another silent thanks to the Universe. Kath was my rock during my dad's passing. I still get reminders of that.

"You know so much was happening so fast, Kath. My head was spinning, I didn't mean to ..."

Kath leans over to me and puts her fingers to my lips. She kisses me and smiles.

“I know,” Kath says and kisses me again. “So what happened after you saw the bank statements and the checks?”

“The multi-tasker in me called my uncle Rob, then the attorney, who advised me to call the police.” I grin at Kath, secretly proud of my repartee, so I mark a point on an imaginary scoreboard just to tease her.

Kath rolls her eyes. “But you didn’t. Right?”

“No, after talking to the attorney, I decided I should head on over to Pop’s house and get the rest of the paperwork, credit card statements and such, while Mary was still at the hospital and before she found out I knew about the checks. God only knows what else she could have been helping herself to.”

“Oh, yeah. That’s when you called me.”

“No, I think I called you after I went to the house.” I respond quickly. “That’s when I found the list Pops made of what Mary inherited when he died—the list had clearly been altered after it had been written. And it wasn’t my dad’s handwriting.”

“Your poor dad.” Kath says as her voice tails off. “I remember you telling me that she was on him mercilessly to sell the house before he went back into the hospital. It gives me the creeps to think about it.”

“When I am tempted to beat myself up for not intervening, I am reminded my job was to love and support Pops—regardless of the choices he made, even the ones I didn’t agree with.”

"That's easier said than done." Kath reflects.

"I'm getting better. The truth is I am at peace when I remind myself I honored my dad by being straight with him. I expressed concern over Mary. He wasn't blind to her neediness, she was clearly pressuring him—but when it was all said and done, he chose to avoid the issues with her as much as he could."

A moment of inspiration hits me as different work scenarios flash through mind like previews at a movie theatre. Frank and I had been going round and round lately. We'd agree to a course of action, and at some point he'd veer off course. I seemed to be going out of my way to remind him of what we were supposed to be doing. I was off the mark. I needed to be straight with him. Either he meant what he said or he didn't. If he changed his mind, then fine—just tell the executive team. It's a basic way of respecting and honoring people. So simple, and it would keep the self-created energy leaks to a minimum.

"Jim?"

"Sorry Kath, I just had to make a mental note of something."

"Ah, the multi-tasker is still at work." Kath says and marks a point on her own imaginary scoreboard.

Now it is my turn to roll my eyes.

"Anyway," I feign annoyance at Kath's comment, "When I finally got back to the hospital, after being at the bank and the house, Mary was sitting in a chair in the corner of the room. I was so angry I couldn't even look at her. I went to Pops bedside and she came over to the bed. I know she was chatting on and on at me, but I kept my eyes on Pops and prayed for guidance. Thank goodness the doctor came in the room and gave us the update on his condition."

"Sometimes they recover, but don't get your hopes up. There is only so much medicine can do." Kath parrots the doctor's prognosis I had shared with her.

"I can't tell you how badly I felt for you at the moment." Kath says. "My heart was breaking for you."

"I know," I say. "I know."

"After I spoke to you, I called my uncle Rob again and then Mike. While Rob and my dad are brothers, they are so different—you know he is fifteen years younger than my dad." I remind Kath. "I can't tell you how much it meant to me when he expressed his faith in me to handle all of this. And Mike, well you know Mike."

"In case I haven't told you," Kath says, "I really like Mike, he's good for you. I can see how close you guys are."

"You know, it's amazing." I tell Kath. "We knew each other in high school but didn't really hang out together until college. We became close through a mutual friend. Ever since, we've been like brothers. It's a truly authentic friendship."

"Yeah, I guess he was just waiting for your big head to shrink some." Kath makes another imaginary point on her scoreboard. I ignore the jest, but smile.

"Between my conversations with you, Rob, and Mike, I decided I wouldn't confront Mary. I still didn't know what to do though, so I put a 911 call to Karen. She helped me get clarity on the basic principle of Trust. She reminded me that I didn't have to know at that moment what to do, I just need to stay the course I was on of honoring my father, not leaking energy by looking for drama over what was legal—I needed to simply trust the answers would come when I needed them."

Kath's quizzical look stops me. She hasn't always liked the concept of my work with Karen. To be fair to her, Kath often says the same things as Karen, with different words of course. I have come to understand Kath's annoyance at the appearance that I listen to Karen but not to her. This is something I've worked on lately.

"It's fine," Kath offers as if reading my mind. "I'm thankful for your growth, Jim."

"Thank you." I say choked up. "It means the world to me that you know how much I have worked on me so we can have a happy, sustainable life together."

Kath takes my hand in hers. We sit quietly together and I can feel the love embracing us.

After a few minutes, I continue.

"The next morning, I got to the hospital early—before Mary would be there. I wanted time alone with Pops. Even though he was in a coma, I needed to be alone with him. I had also called Rob on the way over to the hospital, and asked him to meet me there. I thought it would help to have a third party present and diffuse the tension when Mary arrived." I pause and take a deep breath. It seems impossible to remember without reliving events. It has been almost a year since Pops passed; the pain of grief is easing but not gone.

I take another deep breath and remember my dad's Love. I'm still amazed at the power of my mind. Where I send my thoughts, so too my energy follows. Thank you, God.

"Rob arrived shortly after I did," I continue.

"Rob told me at your dad's service he would never forget entering the hospital room that morning, and watching you hold your dad's hand. He said he was so moved to see you with tears rolling down your cheek," Kath mentions.

I inhale deeply and whisper, "I was just praying for help to endure."

"Yes, Mary was going to be difficult."

"No, my prayer wasn't about Mary. I was praying for the strength to say goodbye. I didn't know if I could let Pops go by agreeing to turn off the life support."

"You know your dad didn't want to linger on life support," Kath says tenderly as she rubs my back.

"Yes, thank goodness Pops made "no lingering" clear. Saying goodbye was difficult enough. But when Rob came into the room, my tears were equal part thank you tears and goodbye tears. I didn't know if Pops could hear me, but I wanted him to know how much I loved him. I wanted him to know I knew he enriched my life. It was hard to put my gratitude for all he taught me into words. Mostly, I wanted him to know he would always live on in our hearts: his humor, the way he always made time for people...he was a sincere man."

"Sincerity runs in the family, at least on your dad's side," Kath says and kisses me again. "I loved the eulogy you gave Pops, Jim. From his funny bone to the way he deeply cared about others. You did a wonderful job speaking from the heart."

"You know, Kath, I was tested that day in the hospital in ways I would never have dreamed possible." I take a moment to let straggling remnants of anger dissipate. I am reminded that we are defined by our choices and powerful people don't make choices in anger.

"No one blames you for being angry, Jim."

"Oh, I don't feel bad at all about being angry. I know my anger is a normal human response. It's just that I......I..."

"You what?"

"I didn't want to make choices or act from that place of anger." I tell her as I observe a crashing wave hit the shore. "When Pops got home from his first hospital stay, he said, "It's all you now, Jim. Not your sisters, not Rob. Just you." I felt like he anointed me as the new head of the family, and I had a responsibility that morning at the hospital to demonstrate family values rather than anger."

"Was Rob still there when Mary came in the room?"

"Yes, and Val."

"It's a good thing your sister is a nurse and could translate the medical jargon about your Dad's condition."

"Even better, Val and I have come a long way. In many ways, my dad brought us back together." I proudly highlight to Kath. I grab my Rum Runner as another point of gratitude emerges.

"What did Val say about Mary taking the money?" Kath inquires.

"I hadn't told her yet. Val was the health proxy and point person with the doctors regarding whether or not he was going to remain on life support. It was hard for all of us, but Val especially."

"That was a heavy burden to carry by yourself, Jim."

"Strangely, I didn't feel by myself. That amazes me even today. Anyway, Mary was the last to arrive. We were saying our goodbyes; the room was somber but full of love for Pops. Then Mary arrived. The energy instantly dissolved. The more she gushed about how much she loved Pops and how much he loved her, the more my stomach turned. I had to step out for a minute to keep my anger in check. It was tough. Real tough."

Taking another sip of my drink, I search within for the sting of my anger. I allow an inner smile to emerge, as I can no longer feel the anger.

"The doctor and nurses came in, and went over the process for turning off life support. Mary wailed some more and made her way to the window. Val, Rob, and I reached out for Pops hands. We encircled him with our Love. I told Pops he was right. It was all me now, and he didn't have to worry—I did have it. Kath, you might think I'm nuts, but I could feel a presence—joyful, loving, peaceful. Pops took a deep breath in and a tear rolled from his closed left eye; I swear he told me "Yes." Yes, he knew I had it now, and he could make his transition in peace. Then he did. So quiet; so peaceful. So much love in the room."

Kath's eyes lock mine; she has tears streaming down her cheeks. I continue to comfort both her and me.

"I was thankful Pops didn't linger. I was amazed at how quickly he passed."

"That was a blessing, Jim. When I think of JoAnn…." Kath's voice cracks. I can sense she is agonizing over JoAnn's suffering; her daughter's suffering, as well as her husband suffering. We were all devastated.

"I know. Fucking cancer," is all I can manage in response. It seems wrong in this day and age for cancer to be a death sentence. Just wrong. Kath lets me know she doesn't want to talk about JoAnn, with a question: "So what happened next with Pops?"

I decided to return to the subject of Pops. At least some of it made sense to me—he was seventy-five, not forty-something like JoAnn. He lived his full life, not half of it.

Dutifully, I answer Kath. "After the doctor pronounced Pops' time of death, Mary rejoined the bedside. She asked if she could have a few minutes alone with him. None of us spoke but we all thought it was peculiar. There were more forms to fill out—endless forms…so we all went to contend with paperwork."

"Remind me to never die," Kath says, lightening the mood.

"You're preaching to the choir," I tell her.

"Almost an hour had gone by while the mortuary arrangements were nailed down when Val told me Mary was still in the room with Pops. I didn't know what Mary was up to so I went back into the room. She turned the tear-ducts up upon my return. I came over to the bed and noticed the ring Pops was wearing was missing. You know the one—the wedding ring from his marriage to Jean. He loved the ring so much that he wore it on his right hand after they divorced. I looked at Mary and noticed she had put the ring on her thumb. I don't know why I was surprised."

"That ……I don't know what to call her," Kath seethes, "but I can't think of anything nice!"

"I think the word you are looking for is Bitch—with a capital 'B'." I quip.

"What did you do?"

"I told her now was not the place or time to have a property discussion. We needed to have a family meeting that included all of us to decide these things."

"What did Mary say?"

"That Pops wanted her to have the ring because she gave it to him!"

"Oh. My, God." Kath's face is frozen in disbelief.

"I wanted to call her a liar and thief—I'd be lying if I said otherwise. But that part of me didn't win. I didn't allow my anger to make the decision. I politely asked for the ring, Mary refused. I picked up her hand and took the ring off her thumb. I firmly told her to come to the house so we could have a family meeting. That's when I called you the second time that morning."

"I was so worried about you, Jim. I guess I wasn't giving you enough credit."

"I was worried about me too," I smile at her. "Yet, somehow I remembered the prayer Karen gave me, *"Dear God, where do you want me to go, what do you want me to do, what do you want me to say and to whom?"* It was my mantra on the drive over to Pops' house. I was pretty calm by the time I got there—I was thinking, "Wow I sure have changed!" As Mike says, the old me would have been a Tasmanian Devil."

"So did you tell Val then? What about your other two sisters, did you tell them?"

"I didn't have time." I respond. "Val, and Liz arrived together. Liz had just arrived from Virginia. Katherine was still on a plane. I arrived minutes after they did and Mary was on my heels. I wanted to get it over with, so I asked everyone to have a seat and I put the bank copies of the checks on the coffee table."

"What did Mary do?" Kath asks.

"No one did anything for a few moments but stare at the checks," I pause as the clarity of the memory hit me. "I told them I was confused. These two checks were written on days Pops had been in the hospital. The signature wasn't his. Mary interrupted me and tried her best to convince all of us that the signatures were most definitely his. I calmly told Mary the folks at the bank felt otherwise. That's when Mary's dramatics erupted."

"Val was describing this to me after your dad's services. It sounded like a bad movie."

"Yeah, Mary began intense rocking in her chair. She started hitting herself, pulling her hair, whispering to herself like she was nuts. You should have seen Val—she immediately transitioned into nurse mode, it was amazing to watch—she handled Mary perfectly. After Val settled Mary, we all decided to leave. I told Mary, as Pops' executor and power of attorney, I would be taking all of Pop's records with me and we would meet again in a few days. Of course you know the rest."

"You handled that second meeting so well Jim. I mean, your sisters knew most of the details by then, everyone was screaming for action."

"Thanks, Kath. You know it was easy to tell Mary she could keep the money she took and the car—as well as any furniture she wanted—if she got out of the house. My dad only wanted to give her thirty days, I decided sixty days was fair, not sure why."

"I don't know that anyone else would have been so generous, Jim. Not to mention you never called the police."

"Mary had spent the money. She paid off her debts knowing she wouldn't be able to keep making payments without Pops giving her the money. In the end, I knew Pops would care far more about how the community he spent his life in remembered him. If I pressed charges, the Mary drama would only take away from his memory and I didn't want that."

"I think you did the right thing, Jim. My question is how did the flames of that memory get rekindled now on our second honeymoon?"

"I know—it's a hellish winter back home. We are on a warm beach...." Kath's look encourages me to continue. "Pops' birthday was coming up. I was thinking I would drive up to Albany with a lawn chair in the trunk and maybe have a beer or two while I chatted with him." I watch Kath for a reaction. She's a far more practical person. I'm the sentimental sap. I wasn't sure what she would say.

"Grief is a long process," Kath sighs, "I hope you'll do what you need to do." A pained look comes across Kath's face and I realize she's probably thinking about JoAnn.

JoAnn was Kath's soul sister. They were best friends since grade school. Kath grew up as the only girl in a family of four brothers. On childhood vacations, Kath would get to bring JoAnn with her. JoAnn was the maid of honor in our wedding and our son's godmother—probably the best godmother anyone could ever ask for. It was an amazing friendship. JoAnn's cancer suddenly returned three months before Pops died. She passed just three weeks before him.

I am about to ask how JoAnn's daughter was doing when Kath stands up. "It's low tide, let's go for a walk."

"That's another thing I love about you," I tell Kath as I reach up from my chair to take her hand. "You always know when to change things up—how about we fool around in that tropical water? After all, its our anniversary."

Kath smiles, "If you're lucky..."

My smile feels as big as my heart as we head off towards the beach hand, in hand.

The rest of our anniversary getaway goes by fast. It isn't until we are on the plane when I realize I never did circle back with Kath about JoAnn, or how her daughter was. *Argh.* Any alone time I had on the trip I spent writing the book. For the supposedly sentimental one, I still get lost in the to-do list. *Time to cleanup,* I coach myself.

"It's been too much heavy energy, Jim." Kath sighs. I wonder if she is going to cry. I notice my own discomfort at the thought of Kath crying in public on the plane. *We are on a stupid plane. We'll never see these folks again. And even if we did, who cares! Jeez, Jim,* I tell myself, *get real.*

Kath expresses the feeling of being pressed like a flower between the bookends of life. First JoAnn, then Pops—and lastly, as if there wasn't enough loss, her dog Riley. Riley was technically the family dog, but everyone knew Riley was Kath's dog. A car hit him when he was just a puppy, and ever since then he lived under Kath's skirts. Not a command was given him that he didn't look to Kath for confirmation to comply.

"Honestly Kath, if it wasn't for my personal practice, I don't know what I'd do. I mean, yes, many details of life right now are sad. Underlying the grief, I feel a sense of peace. I know deep in my soul that while impermanence is the hallmark of life—I'm fully alive now…sometimes…well I hate to admit it, but sometimes I'm shocked I'm doing so well."

Kath's tart "Good for you" reply pulls my mind up short. Karen's *"You have to meet people where they are, Jim,"* realigns my thinking. As a defensive response is rising in my mind, just as quickly it's quieted. *What is this power at work within me?* All of a sudden, a new understanding of compassion floods over me. Kath supports the changes I've made, "The old you was defined by what you did," she said recently, "and the new you defines what you do." Yet, she sometimes seems reserved in her support of my practice. It's a sore spot with me.

"I'm guilty of trying to rush you past your process, Kath. I know it's not the same as mine."

"It's not that simple, Jim."

I stay quiet waiting for her to continue, but she doesn't. The old me would take out the crow bar and go to work. *So I know what not to do* I coach myself. *Yet, I still don't know how to respond.*

Not true, comes to the forefront of my mind. I realize the source of this commentary is new for me—I felt it when I was giving Pops eulogy; I was constantly given exactly the words to say. No struggle, no pondering, just a quiet revelation, perfect in expression. I remember explaining to Karen that I could swear I'd felt a presence as I was giving Pops' eulogy.

Karen said, "Jim, I can't pretend to know what happens after our bodies and our energy part ways. I can tell you that energy never dies. It transmutes, changes form, but never dies. It's a fact science has known for thousands of years."

I smile inwardly at the first lesson Karen gave me in this regard. She asked me to hold up a piece of paper—to my eyes it was just a regular paper. "What do you see?" Karen asked me.

"Uuuuhh paper?" was my feeble reply.

She smiled the smile I would come to call, "grasshopper is going to get schooled" smile. Karen spoke softly, "When I see this paper I see a tree, tall and strong. I see roots of the tree penetrating deep into the earth. I see soil, rich with the pungent aroma of decay giving way to new life. I see the sky and the clouds. I see the rain that encouraged the tree to grow and I see the sun that beckoned to the tree to stretch its limbs to the sky." I'm shaken in that moment at how little I did see. "Each component of energy in the sun and sky and earth have transmuted into what we call tree," Karen continued. "Now put the paper on the ground in your garden and light the paper on fire."

I couldn't imagine where in the world this pyro technique was going; however, my curiosity compelled me to comply. A brief flash and the paper was no more. "It's gone," I told Karen.

"Look again," she encouraged me.

"Okay, there's ashes," I conceded.

"So now your garden has compost material added to it?" Karen questioned.

"Ok, if you say so, sure, it has more compost." I respond.

"Does not that compost become soil?" she asks.

"Well, I guess..." My reply is limp.

"And will not that soil nourish and grow the garden, which will in turn nourish and grow the cells of those beings that consume vegetables from the garden?"

I know Karen is making a big point. I was still so young in my practice then; my mind was slippery. Occasionally, it would blank out; my ego mind trying to block out data that would transform my mind to a tool of Spirit.

"So you are saying energy only changes form, and that means we do to—it's not just paper."

"Very good grasshopper," Karen nods.

I've never wanted to admit just how slippery my mind was back then. Lord, the defenses I had then amaze me today.

Just be quiet, be attentive—not demanding, come my instructions. My monkey-mind *'how do I respond to Kath'* mantra eases a bit. I've noticed the surfacing of my guidance comes from so deep within me, I can't find it's point of origin.

I feel energy siphon-off as I experience the cool feeling at this guidance. I can become so mesmerized by the guidance; it becomes a rabbit hole for me. I realize this guidance is something Karen had been telling me would occur naturally if I just practice. My mind begins to dance around as my thinking mind is engaged, *Oh, I can't wait to tell Karen about this!*

I'm struck by a realization; my thoughts are streaming simultaneously and not colliding. "Newer, larger bandwidth for thoughts emerge when you stay open," Karen's voice echo's in my head. "And if you try to overthink what to say, the bandwidth closes." And just like that it did.

Cold water in my face wouldn't be as harsh as feeling as the bandwidth dissipating. Each thought I think and repeat closes it even faster. I quickly commit my guidance to memory, *Just be quiet—be attentive not demanding. Just be quiet—be attentive not demanding...just be!*

"Jim? Are you having a stroke or something?"

Kath's elbow to my ribs and question break the last of my connection to the guidance.

"Sorry, Kath, I'm fine." Her stare says she doesn't believe me. "I'm working on honoring you. I recognize that I sometimes try to talk you out of your feelings or point of view. I try to solve your problems instead of offering authentic support to you. Then I get upset when you don't handle the problems the way I think you should."

"Really?" she says, "That's interesting. Give me an example."

Without hesitating, I jump in and start listing examples. I let my opinions run loose, simultaneously knowing opinions are not facts. I am reminded of my sessions with Karen. Our conversations flash to mind. Karen is always quick to highlight those moments where I should have shut up. This is probably one of them. My ego telling Kath's ego about problems I think she has and she needs to work on was not my brightest move. It was more like a title of some kind of book on how to ruin a second honeymoon in ten minutes or less.

"You can't honor and judge at the same time, Jim," Karen reminds me. Our egos have an opinion—which in its laziness mistakes for the truth. On one level, your opinion may well be true. On a much deeper level, it's always the habits that have caused what appears to be the 'problem' that needs examining. People who are supported can discover the habits under the symptoms. Then they can change and grow."

Damn it, I smack myself with the thought.

I knew as soon as I told Kath what I thought needs fixing, it was the wrong thing to do; but I couldn't help myself! I am always trying to convince Kath to join a fitness club, take yoga classes; do something. Yes, I think she should exercise more. Shit, so should I. Our lives are so busy and stressful, its hard for either one of us to find the time.

"Why do I have a tendency to still try to 'fix' things?" I ask Karen in our next session. I've made a ton of progress but this habit still lingers. "Maybe it's because I am afraid, I mean, I love Kath more than anything. In fact, I love her more today than I ever have. I'm not just saying that, I really feel it inside. To me, she is more beautiful today than the day I met her. But for some reason, I am really scared. I'm afraid if she doesn't grow with me, we will grow apart. I think I over-compensate for this feeling by trying to fix things...maybe it's a guy thing, I don't know. All I know is every time I try to fix something, I end up complicating it further."

"Let's have a 'do-over,' Jim. Be Authentic, be Honest. What did you want to communicate?" Karen says.

"I love her and want her to be happy."

So if you said, "Kath, I love you and I want you to be happy. I know I have a habit of trying to fix things; I am working on that. I want to be there for you, to support you, tell me how—and then you shut up. You listen. You clarify what she says to be sure you understand. You don't offer fixes, but rather compassion for her experience."

I can feel a lightness return as I tell Karen, "Sure, make it sound that easy!"

"So when will you execute the do-over?" Karen asks.

"When the Universe tells me to," I chirp back.

I can hear Karen smothering a snicker.

"What's that mean?" I question.

"I was just remembering when you were a little grasshopper and you would have answered that question with ten minutes of 'how I need to understand your circumstance better'—so you'd 'educate' me—followed by ten minutes of things you could do to make your situation better—but probably wouldn't work, and finally ten minutes of things you need to find out before you know ten more things you could do!"

Beyond Karen's howling laughter, I think, *Dear God. She's 100% correct.* I'm horrified by the realization I actually used to function that way.

"I just realized I should be dead," I blurt out. "There is no way a human being could leak that much energy, never seeing a return on the investment, and survive."

"That's another testimony to the measure of Goodness in the Universe, Jim. We humans do so many stupid, stupid things—yet in any moment we can be made anew."

Karen has never used words like born again, but she can quote the Bhagavad Gita, the Bible, the Vedas, the Sutra's, the Koran, the Kabala—she's even explained the historical and anthropological contexts of various sacred teachings. Naturally I'm more familiar with Christian terms, yet I know we are not discussing religion—just the message beyond the dogma. I've been feeling a strong pull to begin to investigate various sacred texts and I mention this again.

Karen has made it clear that Love is the only religion anyone needs to ever have. She has also said I need to follow my guidance, in whatever method works for me. I feel a missing piece fall into place as I tell Karen, "I want to know, beyond a shadow of all doubt the ever-present goodness of the Universe. I don't want to live with one foot in the ego sand-box and the other foot on Heaven's doorstep."

"I understand." Karen is quiet. I remain quiet, anticipating more.

"Einstein said there are only two ways to live: as if everything was a miracle, or nothing was a miracle. Buddha said the mind cannot serve two masters. Jesus lived on earth, but thought the thoughts of heaven. The Course in Miracles says the vision of one world costs you the vision of the other."

"Crap, it's going to take me a month to process all of that!" I exclaim.

"I've been processing it for twenty years, Jim." Karen's voice isn't irritated, but there is a gravity to it.

I continue, "So what you are saying is under everything I think, say, or do...damn! I was so close, but the thread just broke, I lost the understanding."

"I'm saying we are wired for the goodness of the Universe. Anything perverse is an invention of our ego mind—and we are bound by the laws of the world we decide to align ourselves with. I tell myself daily "I am under no laws but God's" as an affirmation. Some days I need to remind myself of this truth one hundred times. Does it get easier with practice? Yes, of course, but the ego, in my experience, is never something that goes away. We just develop the power to not let it rule us, or make choices for us."

"What exactly does the ego want?" I notice eagerness welling up, I feel like I'm inches from understanding my life in a completely different way.

"Egos are purveyors of fear. Control freaks. Identified with the impermanent, with thoughts and emotions. Egos are delusional. Egos have a limited use to navigate the world of form, but have gone amuck. Egos are not who we are, they are impermanent, just like our bodies. Egos think you are your body." Karen sighs and continues. "Egos think the purpose of other bodies, objects or sentient beings is to be used or consumed—to the ego nothing is sacred. Egos can't even understand the concept of sacred. The only thing the ego wants is to run the show. To the ego, life is drama. It'll make the stage, sew the costumes, cast the characters—anything to keep the drama going."

"Karen, it feels like a slippery slope to me. Just one thought amiss, leads to another, then another and before I know it my ego gets hooked to something, my fears and worries get going...I know I've made progress—yet I want my ego to go away!"

"I do understand," Karen sympathizes. "In my experience fighting the ego, attempting to banish the ego only creates more ego. Instead, turn your vision away from the ego. Remember the story of Daniel and the Lion's Den in the Bible?" Karen asks.

"Of course," I reply, "Every child in every Sunday School gets that story."

"The lions are a metaphysical symbol for fear. All the imaginings of the ego mind: its worries, its fear, its insanity that life is against you—and in the story the fear life is against Daniel is represented by the lions. Do you remember what Daniel did with the lions?"

"He slayed them?" I ventured.

"He turned his back on them. The lions fell asleep, and he slept with them."

"I need to stop fighting, blaming and judging my ego?" I question

"Simple. Not easy." Karen affirms. "So the do-over with Kathy. All Spirit or Love, no ego or fear. Only the ego has something to defend," Karen reminds me.

As I end my session with Karen, my ego is reminding me my week is already packed—so I shouldn't expect to find the right opportunity for a do-over with Kath.

I sigh. Then shake my head no as I observe every maneuver of my ego. *I can see you,* I tell my ego, a*nd there's nothing to be afraid of.* For the first time ever, I feel a softening towards my ego. *Is this self-compassion,* I wonder?

The Power of the Universe

Taking a week off for my belated second honeymoon was hard. Note to self: *I want vacations to be easy!* I look at my back-to-back meetings for the day and declare to no one there, *"I am under no laws but God's."* I only half believe my declaration when I hear an echo, *"The Universe doesn't need much, just your small willingness."* I close my calendar, close my laptop and breathe my thanks to the Goodness of the Universe for its answer. I can stay willing; I have no doubt about that.

One of my personal "ME INC." items upon my return was to get my 2011 bonus reconciled. No surprise, Frank hasn't mentioned it to me. Pops, JoAnn, and Riley all passed during the fall; I've had a hard time keeping the train on the track at work. February of 2012 is just two days away and I don't have my bonus paid yet. *It's my doing,* I remind myself. *I am responsible for taking care of me.* I feel a surge of willingness to take hold of me like I have never felt before.

I'm proud of the discipline I bring to my practice, *it's just a detail,* I remind myself. *Send the spreadsheet,* I tell myself. *"The numbers are the numbers and everyone should be happy we've had such a good year.* We beat our forecast. We beat our stretch goal. Secretly, I know the margin could have been better, but *Small victories, Big changes* I remind myself. This is all part of the five-year plan. I still hit my kicker—even though Frank thought it would never happen. His mindset can only look at the numbers in front of him today. He can't see the roadmap to the growth number I am projecting. *Oh, well Jim,* I remind myself, *handle the details and leave the rest be. Give it space and see what develops.*

After two days of back-to-back mind-numbing meetings, I decide to work at home on Wednesday. I have a few presentations and customer check-ins to do as well as get my year-end bonus reconciliation finished. I had mentioned to Frank I was working on my bonus reconciliation at the end of our executive staff meeting on Monday. The memory of his returning look kept me awake two nights in a row. Not to mention, Frank has brought up several times, "We need to get your 2012 compensation plan together." I am determined not to repeat the 2011 experience. Frank's been waffling back and forth on the direction of the company. He wants to grow, but doesn't want to make the investment. He wants to cut expenses to show higher margins, but can't cut because 100% of the resources are being used. Frank is schizophrenic in his desires, which will make negotiations for a compensation plan insane.

"Okay, I know monkey-mind is at work here." I say out loud. *My ego keeps telling me to be worried.* Karen would say to honor myself, be honest about how I feel, then look past it to what my Spirit would say.

"Step one is....is....align with my intention!" I blurt out. I'm glad no one else is home or I'd feel silly. "My intention is...." I'm faltering as the ego is vomiting predictions on the theme: "He's not going to pay you."

Screw it, I tell myself. I rarely make 911 calls to Karen, and she has always said if I need to—I should. As I dial her number I rationalize she'll be busy and probably won't be able to answer immediately, but she'll get back to me....

"Oh hey, I'm shocked I got you on the phone, I thought I'd be leaving a message," I blurt out as Karen answers.

"Hi Jim," Karen's voice is light; I always admire the joy I feel coming from her. "As a matter of fact, I have a client who cancelled at the last minute—the Universe must have known you need me!"

"I love the Universe!" I say in relief. She doesn't say anything, but she doesn't have to, I know I've got the green light to spit it out. "My monkey-mind is jumping and swinging in the trees! I know in my gut Frank is going to try to cheat me out of my bonus. I can feel it."

I rehash the immense data file my monkey-mind has stored. The games Frank played with the wording of my compensation plan. The obtuse nature of its structure—the many times I needed to get clarification. Random sentences poured out of my mouth, as I told her the way he responded to my attempts at clarification with bullshit like, "Jim, relax, jeez it's like you don't trust me." As I'm dumping the history, I notice I'm getting angry with myself because Frank's tactics did work to some degree to shut me up. My bonus gets paid on gross revenue, not net. I have no doubt that Frank and I are on the same page with the parameter of gross revenue—yet my ego can see Frank using the lack of clear wording in the written agreement to his advantage.

"Anything else you need to tell me?" Karen asks.

"Karen, if you saw the look on his face Monday when I told him I was doing the 2011 bonus reconciliation I know you'd agree with me. Something is up!"

"Jim, my ego mind agreeing with your ego mind is hardly helpful."

"I know. But I don't want to be crazy about this." I snapped back.

"So then don't be! Jim, what is your intention?"

"I want him to pay me!"

"So you want him to give you money just because?" Karen inquires.

"No! Of course not! I earned that money. I deserve that money."

"Oh, I see," Karen says softly "You want an equitable exchange for the value you provide that honors both you and the company which has already been agreed to."

"Okay, smarty pants," I say lightening up. "I get your point."

"Now you have a clear articulation of your intention," Karen continues. "What is step two?"

"Tell him, speak to the heart of the matter—without monkey-mind judgment."

"Yes, I like to say it more as an affirmation. Affirmations are proactive."

"Keep going." I implore Karen

"Try: "Frank, as you know we spent considerable time on my compensation plan. Our goal was to establish an equitable exchange for the value I provide. I've just finished reconciling the numbers; I've hit my kicker, which means the company has done really, really well. It's a win-win!"

"So I should just ignore my gut?"

"No, Jim. You don't ignore it. You ask the Universe for guidance. Until it gives you clear instructions as to Frank's intentions, you don't have useful information to move you forward."

"But that is so...."

"Hard?" Karen finishes my thought.

"Your damn right this is hard!" I stress.

"Take a breath, Jim. Move to the higher level of sight. Your ego may be right. In fact, I'd bet it's right. But you don't have any power engaging Frank or fighting with him. Your power is with the alignment of your intentions. That is where the Universe supports you—not in reactive behaviors, but in responsive behaviors."

"Something just occurred to me. I know everything you are saying, Karen. I've been in this lesson before."

Karen signals I've understood something significant with her "Ding, Ding, Ding!" response.

"So what is it? What is it that I am not getting?"

"Jim, that's an ego perspective. 'I must be doing something wrong or I wouldn't need to repeat this lesson. The last time you worked with this part of your practice, you did so on the level of your understanding at the time. The stakes were "smaller," according to how the ego frames "small" and "big." Now, according to the ego the stakes are huge—about half of your annual compensation—yes?"

"Just about," I affirm.

"So according to how the ego operates, it should jump in and run the show now because the stakes are so big. The ego is disclosing one of its primary illusions to you, Jim—the ego believes there is an order of difficulty in the power of the Universe...."

"Ding, Ding, Ding!" I jump ahead of Karen and finish her sentence, "Is the Universe, omnipotent and omnipresent or is it only kinda, sorta, sometimes powerful?"

"Amen!" Karen exclaims with a chuckle, "Let the choir sing!"

"So basically, I've said I want a connection to the Universe—to know it's goodness all the time, but that is impossible if I don't truly Trust it. If I believe it doesn't have the power my experience has confirmed it has."

"Jim! I am so, so, so happy for you. I can't tell you the number of folks I work with who take decades to get that. They say they believe in the power of the Universe, but don't really. Congratulations. Hang onto that understanding. Write it down, read it several times a day."

"I just remembered something you told me over a year ago—I knew it was important, but didn't get it. In fact I was reading my notes from our old sessions this morning and saw it: There is no such thing as a faithless person. Either you believe in the power of the three dimensional world to keep you down in some way, or you believe in the power of the Universe to lift you up. We have faith in the disease. We have faith in the bad economy; we have faith in all things ego made..."

"The vision of one world costs you the vision of the other." Karen finishes.

"Ahhhh, yes, now I understand. I mean, I'm not just saying it Karen, I really understand now."

"That is precisely why I am over joyed, Jim."

"Okay, I know it's monkey-mind—but it's screaming I have to do something about my bonus."

"Is there anything within your own mind that says you didn't provide an equitable exchange?" Karen asks.

"Absolutely not. Even though there are times Frank isn't capable of seeing the value I bring to the table, I know he would be one of the first ones to admit that I do."

"Okay then, lean into the power of what is: the company has done well for the last three years in a supposedly terrible economy in large part thanks to your leadership. You are simply asking for what you are entitled to. Can you feel the peace underlying the Truth?"

"I was just going to mention I resonate with that...."

"Good. If you want to send me a draft of the email to Frank to be sure you keep the train on the tracks, feel free."

"I can't thank you enough Karen. This was big today."

"In more ways than you know, Jim." Karen finishes. I don't want to hang up the phone. Of course more is stirring in the Universe than my human eyes perceive, Karen just reminded me of that. It's actually exciting—exciting to know that big changes are in the future, and I need to only do my part.

"I'm Trusting," I cheerfully announce and just to be sure I carry the thought with me, I repeat it, "I'm Trusting."

While I'm tempted to check email and check voice mail *(good lord, my phone rang four times while I was speaking with Karen!)*, I know better. It's the slippery slope of ego thinking and I am not going to let it have one moment—at least not until I get the email to Frank finished and sent. I keep it simple and speak from my heart: I'm grateful he has had so much faith in me to allow me to make the changes that have supported the company's growth. I'm even happier we beat the revenue numbers we dreamed about when he hired me, and know if we keep it up we will continue the growth into 2012 and beyond. I'm proud of myself for drafting a separate email to the bookkeeper, copying Frank, requesting information on dates the bonus checks will be cut. The bookkeeper can take care of the details with Frank. Keeps it nice and clean for me, and that is, after all her job.

My email doesn't mention my ego's problem with Frank's inconsistency. *I know instead of beating the stretch goal by $800K, we could have beat it by millions—if he would just stop mucking up the waters.* "Say what you mean, and mean what you say," has been one of the early mantras Karen gave me that is still with me every meeting I have with Frank. *Hold it right there!* I've caught myself; the slippery slope of ego thinking awakens me. I take a breath, another, inhale to the count of one—two—three—four—and exhale to the count of one—two—three—four. *Yup that did the trick, the ego hook is gone.*

I didn't believe it when Karen first told me that seventeen seconds is ALL that is required to let the ego hook go—if you do not keep re-thinking the thought! Just one more of my old ego habits I can easily quell now. The umbrella of Peace is surrounding me as I recognize the progress I've made will serve to keep the upcoming storm at bay.

Within two hours of sending my bonus reconciliation email to Frank and the second email to the bookkeeper requesting notification of the dates the bonus checks would be cut. I'm texting Karen furiously:

"911. Check your email. Forwarded BS response re: bonus."

Karen's reply is firm: "Yup saw it. Make two lists—one what ego says, other what Spirit says. Call tomorrow at 6am."

I'm not happy with Karen's response. I want to do something—anything—NOW. *Damn that motherfucker—he's trying to cheat me. The bookkeeper would not have sent the response she did without consulting Frank.* Reading the response a second and third time inflames me further. She strikes a tone that is not appropriate for my rank. *I'm the COO, and she is speaking down to me.* "Sorry you have your numbers wrong. Here's what actually came in." *Does she think I'm a fucking idiot?*

Wait. I coach myself. Karen gave me homework. There has never been a piece of homework she has given me that has been a waste of my time. In fact the opposite—I can discern what I could not previously understand prior to completing the homework. *Okay, unplug from the office and do the homework,* I command myself. I notice my ego wants to continue to howl at the situation. So I start with that list first. My ego is furious and wants to figure out how to force Frank to give me what is mine. My ego is pissed off—for creating this energy leak in my life. My ego wants to quit. Right now, leave him high and dry—who cares. My ego wants to tell everyone and anyone—expose the ugly truth. Mostly, my ego is scared shitless. It has no idea what to do next, although ego seems willing to do anything half cocked and blind with condemnation.

I take a breath. I notice my asthma is acting up. It's no wonder. Extreme stress is not good for asthma. Clearly I have worked myself, *with good reason, I console myself,* into a Tasmanian Devil tizzy.

Might as well do the other list now, comes clear guidance. *Well, duh, won't do any good,* my ego answers guidance.

My mood is dark, and foul, and I resist being lifted up. "Interesting," I say to no one in particular—but just in case the Universe is going to pull a miracle, I summon a half-hearted, "I'm Trusting."

My list from Spirit reminds me of the unlimited abundance of the Universe. My gain doesn't come from another's loss. (Ego chirps Frank will see paying my bonus as a loss for him.) Spirit reminds me of my intention, an equitable exchange for the value I provide, and Spirit reminds me I am under the laws of the world I decide to have faith in. I know my emotions are normal, human, and even Karen wouldn't fault me for them. But they trick my mind into looking only at the ego's world, which is most definitely not the world I have power in, nor want to have faith in.

So it's that simple, I can move forward in Trust that if I do my part in the present moment the Universe will do its part. I feel a modicum of Peace return and my gratitude swells as I realize the point of my homework. *I have a well-established practice! I need more patience, I need to turn to my practice (that is the Discipline, Karen would remind me)*; *stay with it*—but mostly just work through the steps. *It's all within: my connection to the Universe and the answers I need.*

I've been staring at the picture I took of the Adirondack Mountains on the family trip from a couple years ago as I work through my steps. I notice is seems to come alive. It's more vibrant, and while it has always called to me *(which is why I framed it and hung it in my office),* there is another message now. I decide to just meditate on the picture and invite guidance. In a blink I see a hiking path on the mountain. I never really noticed it before—it's faint but as many times as I have looked at the picture, the paths have escaped my notice.

The path encircles the mountain. Each circle of the path is a bit higher up the mountain then the previous circle. In another blink I'm struck. *I do the same thing with my practice. I'm summiting and circling back to the Spiritual Principles of Intention, Openness, Peace, Unhooking, Alignment, Clarity...*"Wow," I'm speaking to an empty room that feels anything but empty. I can feel the energy shift as I sort through previous lessons on earlier parts of my path. *Karen is dead on, when the stakes are high, our egos want to grab the reins of life.*

It was hard to Trust at times during the drama with Pops' death. Yet every detail worked out better than I could have imagined—with ease and grace. Ego clearly wants to take over based upon believing that it's too important to leave my bonus to chance.

I smile inwardly as I discover a deeper meaning to Karen's question, "How big is the Universe, Jim? Either you believe, as most do, in a kinda, sorta, powerful Divine Intelligence—or you come to understand the Divine Intelligence of the Universe as the power that is ever present, everywhere, all the time. Which you believe will determine the power the Universe has in your life. I don't know about you, but I want more than a parking space from the Universe."

Why do I ask the Universe for so little? I muse. *I'm back to Trust and Surrender,* I remind myself. *Trust and Surrender.*

"Are you awake?" I ask Karen. It's 6 am, the truth be told I've been up for almost two hours. I keep jumping back and forth between knowing the Universe will do a better job at sorting through the complexities of this situation then I will—and my ego wanting to have a show-down at the ok-corral.

"Yes, thanks. I've had a cup of coffee and even managed to get in a nice meditation," Karen answers.

"I want to be able to be that calm—all the time," my words are wistful.

Karen encourages me, "You are getting there, Jim. "

"Here's what I learned," I begin. I know in my heart Trust and Surrender are key here—and my ego keeps hooking back in with 'what to do.'"

"So what does your Spirit want you to do, Jim?"

"Honor and respect myself, keep my word and my agreement, and not engage in any ego drama."

"Bravo! See you didn't need me after all...." Karen is chuckling. "So lets imagine next steps," she continues.

"Acting like everything is normal seems like a betrayal to myself. Honestly, I don't feel like going into the office at all."

"What do we owe another when their word has been broken Jim? Personally, I'm fascinated egos want to bind us to contracts wherein the other person has in fact cancelled the contract by not keeping their word."

"That's it—Frank has broken our contract! I didn't even see that."

"Let me give you an analogy: say a couple is married. A clear part of their vows is to be faithful in all ways to one another. If one violates that vow, they have violated a sacred trust and the marriage agreement. The ego points out "legally" it's still married, but Spirit knows that is not true—the marriage agreement has been cancelled. Hence the agony over "forgiving," as egos usually think it means 'staying' when the marriage, as ego knew it, is over."

"So my relationship with Frank is over?" I probe.

"Yup, it sure is. And the really good news, Jim: if you choose to have a new relationship with Frank, you get to consciously define the terms of the new relationship."

"I would like that! I would really like that." I answer.

Do you want to be in the position that you are chasing Frank for money again?"

"Hell no," I quietly respond.

"So you have been saying for months that you want to launch your own company again."

"Yes, I've said that a million times!"

"Don't you think Divine Intelligence has given you the ticket to do just that?"

"What do you mean? You lost me."

"There are two parts to what is in front of you: the money and your future relationship. They are related." Karen emphasizes.

"Yes, because I need a new compensation plan for this year..." The fixation Frank has had on my 2012 comp plan, coupled with his schizophrenic expressions of what he wants from me come flooding into my mind.

"And you can't make new agreements until the old one is settled," Karen finishes.

"I'm supposed to have a meeting with Frank today about my 2012 comp plan!" I can feel the excitement building. Not ego excitement, but reassurance of Spirit—there is a plan. The Universe is supporting me. I continue, "So I can meet with Frank, explain that we need to get some cleanup done around 2011 before we can move on to 2012."

"Exactly," Karen concurs.

"My monkey-mind is screaming 'HOW?'" I exclaim.

"Let it be easy. First I note in his email back to you..." I cut Karen off—she's a little confused about who sent the email: it is, after all, only a few minutes past 6 am.

Karen laughs and continues, "Jim, if Frank didn't write that email and have the bookkeeper send it, I'm the pope." Karen's words hit me deeply.

"Of course!" I yell. "Now her tone, which totally annoyed me, makes sense because it wasn't her tone!"

"See, this is the problem with ego, Jim. It assigns actions and motives to fill in gaps of information. Tell me, has the bookkeeper ever, and I mean ever, been less than courteous, helpful, and open to you?"

"Never. She has never hinted at rude or unhelpful responses."

"So what sense would it make for her to start?"

"Now I feel like a jerk, I've been cursing her out in my mind for a day." I confess.

"Self-condemnation is not the point of seeing with Spirit, Jim. Just observe the ego, smile, and respond to it like you do a small child playing with its food. Ego doesn't know any better than the child."

"Thanks for the reminder—hey! I just got a download. Karen, this is so cool—I think I should go into the bookkeeper's office and connect on the basis of our actual experience with one another and tell her I am surprised she wrote the email for Frank. Let her know I am not upset with her, but surprised as it didn't seem like her."

"Excellent. Next will be cleanup with Frank. Do not allow yourself to be moved along in conversation until Frank completely admits he wrote the email, forced the bookkeeper to send it to you with her name on it, and is in fact manipulating the data to get out of paying you." Karen accentuates.

"I know that's what I have to do. I gotta tell you, Karen, I'm uneasy about it. What if Frank..." I stop myself. *I know any worry or fear I have is ego monkey-mind.*

"Jim, stay in your power—just like you did with Mary stealing the money from your dad," Karen reminds me.

"It's true, I didn't know how I stayed so calm; the speed of the resolution was a miracle."

"No engagement of egos—only a clear communication from you to Frank: 'We can't move on and discuss anything else until this is cleaned-up.'"

"Listen, I know Frank is going to tell me not to worry, we'll fix it and skip over it. I do not want to get triggered and say something out of integrity for me."

"Why can't you move on until this is clarified?"

"I think that is what Frank would say!" I exclaim loudly. *It's still early in the house and I've been trying to not wake anyone.*

"I have all day," Karen says with a sing-songy vocal tone that I translate into meaning I need to answer the question as she isn't changing subjects. My brain feels like it's going to explode when the self-apparent answer becomes obvious to me:

"Because I don't trust him!"

"It's that simple, Jim. He wants to make new agreements with you. Any agreement would require trust. If he wants new agreements, he needs to re-establish trust by telling the truth."

"I guess this is a perfect example of the answers being present, and it's only my ego mind that would obscure them."

"Exactly—again!" Karen hoots.

I hear Kath coming down the stairs, then her question, "Jim, is everything okay?"

I tell her just a minute, I'm almost done, when Karen interrupts me, "Jim, just a reminder, don't be the old you with Kathy. Think about 'both-and' not 'either-or.' Be determined to practice 'all things are for your good.'"

"I'm ahead of you there, I already made up mind to do just that."

"Excellent," Karen responds. "I look forward to hearing about your success."

I'm holding up one finger to Kath, as I finish thanking Karen for her help. As soon as I hang up I let Kath know that everything is actually okay, even though it may not look like it. Kath's puzzled look is the perfect segway into offering her a cup of coffee and a seat at the kitchen table so I can tell her what is happening.

"Jim, I'm not sure I get what you are saying. Are you going to quit today?"

"Kath, I don't know what is going to happen today. I only know I can't get ahead of myself. I need to do each step, fully, with the intention of honoring myself and remaining unhooked from any ego crap. If I get triggered by anything, I need to move quickly into a higher vision of what really is happening."

"Jim, I want you to be happy. I don't want you to be mistreated, but I'm scared."

"Kath, there is some cleanup I've needed to do with you. I can't move forward without your support. I know I've communicated my meaning over the last week poorly. All I want is for you to be happy too. I'm scared you are not happy so I keep offering suggestions, which I do mean as helpful—but the truth is there is fear entangled in the suggestions. Fear you blame me, fear I could or should be doing something to help you and I am not."

"I guess I'm more private about my struggles than you are. No, I don't think that is all of it—I think it's that I don't have words to describe how I feel at times. Yes, there is grief—but it's something beyond that. I'm just not sure what is going to happen next. I'm probably not making sense now..."

I give Kath a big hug. We hold each other for a few moments. I notice the picture of the mountain and the path circling up to the summit. *The illumination of my experience, my seeking a better way is plain and clear.*

"Kath, you remember a few years ago when I was wrapping up the buy-out of my last company?" I don't wait for an answer. I know she does. "I was driven, crazy and blind with fear. My playbook—my certainty factor—was an illusion. I always thought I knew what was going to happen next, I was so confident my intelligence, my persistence; my drive would always be enough. When everything began to come apart, hell when Kevin and I began to come apart, I had to admit that my playbook only took me so far. I could no longer deny the control over the world I thought I had was an illusion. Life was uncertain and I was crushed."

I let the gravity of my words settle in her heart before I go on.

"I hid my misery by doing and then doing more."

"I hide my misery with a glass of wine, chocolate, or hallmark movie." Kath offers.

"And the truth is neither of us needs to hide our misery. We love each other, we need to connect beyond egos talking and explaining what we think—we need to be honest about our experience in life."

Kath takes a deep breath, and fixes her gaze directly on me. "What makes you so certain everything is going to be fine now?"

"Because I'm not trying to make anything happen. I am trusting that if I do my part, the Universe will do its part—and whatever that part is—it will be exactly what is needed."

"So your playbook is out the window?"

"Yes."

"Is that how you handled your dad, sisters, Mary—so well?"

"Yes."

"It's hard to argue with proof right in front of your face," Kath smiles at me. "Whatever happens today, I support you. Go get 'em—or whatever one says when you are…."

"Allow," I interject. "It's a process of allowing. Letting the help in, receiving the help, keeping monkey-mind in check to not screw up the help."

"I'll be honest, I'm a little nervous, but I trust you—always have." Kath thoughtfully takes the last sip of her coffee, puts her cup down, and kisses me on the cheek. I hear my son up and moving about, getting ready for school. The day is moving on and I'm welcoming it.

"Thanks, babe! I really mean that. I love you. I love the way we have grown together—especially given everything that has happened; it means a lot. Thanks for being my wife."

Kath smiles, touches my face and begins to get ready for work.

Three hours after my call with Karen I'm sending an update: The bookkeeper fell apart crying the minute I put the printed email on her desk. I didn't have to speak a word—she felt terrible, couldn't sleep. She was furious. Frank made her send it; she said she protested. She told me she was looking for another job, that this was the last straw."

Two hours later I'm relaying that Frank has had something come up and needs to reschedule lunch. I left the office, and don't plan on answering the phone, emails, nada. I'm staying unplugged and unhooked. I will not engage on the ego level.

"Good for you!" is Karen's response.

Six pm and Greg is calling me. I don't answer, but listen to his voice mail. *I wonder what Frank has said to him.*

"Jim, what is going on? Frank said some weird things to me, I'm sure he's made some royal missteps if you are this pissed at him. I don't know the details, so I'm a little confused. Need anything, just call."

Greg has integrity. I'm thankful for that. I wonder what I could tell him that wouldn't suck him into this mess. I want the issues to stay where they are: between Frank and I. I decide to call him back—don't want him to think I am upset with him in any way. I also have nothing to hide. I haven't done anything wrong.

"Christ Jim, it's unbelievable—I mean I didn't think Frank would stoop that low," Greg blurts out after I finish relaying events. "And by the way," he adds, "I saw the bookkeeper—she is still so shaken up. She's afraid she will lose her job now."

I'm grateful to the Universe for that piece of information. I resolve to move forward aware of my commitment to avoid collateral damage. I let Greg know I will not be connecting with anyone in the office until this matter is settled with Frank.

Greg answers, "Jim, everyone knows you. They know if you can be treated like this, so can they."

"Wait, how do people know what happened? I have not spoken to a soul—except the bookkeeper and she already...never mind. I answered my own question: if she's upset like you say, she's re-telling the events...."

"Bingo," Greg answers. "Jim, I'm nervous. Without you the company is in trouble. You are the filter and buffer that keeps all our good talent here and not circulating their resumes."

"Thanks, Greg. I appreciate it. I'm doing each step, one at a time—and not steering to a destination other than honoring myself, an equitable exchange for my value with no drama. On the no drama end, I would appreciate it if Frank approaches you again, please refer him back to me. You don't belong triangulated in this."

"Let's talk soon," Greg offers.

Another day passes, the emails are flying, voicemail keeps beeping indicating another urgent business challenge needs to be solved. I feel at peace sidelined. I remind myself there is nothing for me to do until the Universe guides me.

Greg sends me a text, "Just told Frank to work it out with you ASAP as this doesn't concern me."

I send a prayer of gratitude for Greg's integrity and another sign from the Universe that all is unfolding as it needs to.

I can't decide if I should leave my email closed and check in the morning, or check a few times this evening. I must look like I'm conflicted, as Kath asks me what I am thinking about. After I explain my conflict, she asks, "What would make you happy?"

"To honor myself." I have to marvel at the sound of this, things really are that simple. Karen's reminder that fear is a poor guide helps me close my computer and leave email for the morning.

Friday morning arrives, my peace is undisturbed—I've slept well. I don't know what is going to happen next, but I did decide I wouldn't work in this kind of environment any longer. I value myself. *Surprisingly, valuing myself has kept monkey-mind quiet. I guess it doesn't know how to respond to that!* I laugh at myself while making coffee and ask myself what I should do next. I've cycled through the anger and frustration. *I don't think I can remember the last time I was that angry.*

I've come through the transition of monkey-mind chatter and ensuing energy leaks and now I've made my peace. Frank has done what he has done, and I can only move forward. So forward it is: I decide to check emails.

There are several voicemails and emails from Frank. Even one from the bookkeeper letting me know that Frank is shocked I am so calm. Frank wants to meet Monday for dinner, "To work everything out." I know I want to spend my session with Karen on this, and I want to continue to honor myself and process what I need to so I can meet with Frank and still be the kind of person I want to be—respectful, honest, and honoring of myself, and others. I decide to let Frank know I wasn't available Monday, but was Tuesday.

Frank confirms within five minutes. *Maybe I'm still absorbing the shock—maybe my practice is working—whatever it is, I am light all weekend and my power is returning.* I've managed to plug the massive energy leak. A clear sign my power has returned is writing my blog post, "Be true to yourself." It came with the ease and grace only the Universe provides.

I spend time sorting the file of my dad's affairs. Looking back, I could see ease and grace had their hands on every action item and step with Pops' passing and ensuing events. *When I needed assistance, Mike or Rob stepped up. The house sold easily, Mary is out (with no drama), and my sister took care of the remaining furniture.* Reviewing the trajectory of the events with Pops and Mary, there is no way any ego mind would believe this resolution was possible. I smile at my timing. *The file had been sitting on my desk for months—just waiting for me.* I understand why I answered the call to sort it this morning: all the proof any ego could ever need the Universe is good is right here.

"Just Trust," I say out loud. "Just Trust."

Monday I let Karen know I want to focus on Tuesday's dinner—but I also want to spend time reviewing the first part of the book. She suggests we come up with a plan to handle the book separately and honor the process I am in now. "For all you know, Jim, you are living chapters in the book now."

"So true," I agree.

I give Karen an update on my process so far, where my head is at in the moment. *I'm surprised I am willing to walk away, but it's the truth so I don't hide it.*

"Jim, you don't need to sabotage yourself, or worry about the outcome." Karen begins.

"I had a cool reminder of that over the weekend." I share with Karen my big picture view of my cleanup with Pops' file.

"Way cool," Karen hums. "So let me be sure I understand what you've said: you don't want to engage Frank on any level—other than an honest one."

"Exactly."

"Okay, then your meeting is simple on Tuesday. That is all you have to say. You have no numbers to defend, they are what they are and either Frank keeps his word or he doesn't—but you are fine either way."

"Clarity begets simplicity," I reflect to her.

"Einstein said when the solution is simple, God is calling," Karen adds. "It's only ego minds that love complication."

"Do you mind if I call you on the way over to dinner Tuesday? You know, just for a tune up if I need it?"

"I'd be upset if you didn't." I can feel Karen's smile over the phone.

Walking into dinner Tuesday night is surreal. Kath has given me the biggest vote of confidence and support. Karen is supporting me by reminding me of my own experience with Trust and Surrender, "You don't need to worry about what others do—just what you do." I do feel fine. I'm committed to an honest conversation.

When I arrive, Frank's smile is awkward. He tries his staple 'let's get a drink so we can talk' greeting. I order water and he gives me a double take. He orders his scotch on the rocks. I listen to him for a few minutes and then I'm compelled to stop him.

"Frank, I'm not willing to sit here all night and dance around the issue. The only thing I am willing to do right now is have an honest conversation." I put the email from the bookkeeper on the table. Frank knows what it is and squirms.

"Why did you have someone else send this email to me? What is your intention?"

Of course Frank doesn't answer; he dances around and around. *It's painful to watch really. He could have peace if he just admitted his mistake—but he is hooked by his ego rationalizing, minimizing, and blaming others.* That's when I stop him again.

"Frank, I will need to go if we can't get to the truth." *I know Frank is aware the bookkeeper told me the truth.* She told me herself that she told Frank she has come clean with me. I refuse to have collateral damage and bring her up. I eye Frank and watch him squirm.

"Okay, I made her send the email," he snaps at me. "There, now are you happy?"

"No, I am not happy. In fact, I'm sad. I don't know how to work in a situation where I can't trust. Do you know how?" I'm surprised by the ease with which the words roll off my tongue. No sharp edges to cut into his ego; just sincere speaking from the heart.

"How can we move forward, Jim?" Frank looks like he has more to say, so I am quiet. "It's just that the numbers are complicated," he adds.

"Frank, again: I will not have a dishonest conversation. You said you want to move forward. Being honest is the only way we can move forward together."

"I think we have a misunderstanding about how your commission is paid…" At that, I breathe in deeply, take a drink of my water, and stand up.

Frank quickly asks me to sit down and says he'll pay me the money, "No need to worry about that."

The waiter comes over and says our table is ready. I excuse myself to go to the restroom and tell Frank I'll meet him at the table. In the bathroom, I regroup. I can feel my anger rising at each maneuver Frank executes. I do not want to act out of anger I remind myself. I pull the coin from my pocket I've been fumbling with. On one side, it says "Clarity." *Yes,* I silently agree. *Time for clarity on exactly how Frank is going to pay me.*

The tension feels lighter when I sit at the table. A menu is in front of me, but I don't pick it up. Frank inquires what I am going to have.

"Frank, I'm not sure I'll be staying for dinner. But you go ahead," I answer him.

He confesses he hasn't planned on such a large bonus to me so cash is an issue. I suggest he pay me over time. Frank asks for a ten-month payout. *I'm not sure why, but I'm fine with it.* I tell Frank I'll write up our agreement; he'd have it in his inbox by 7 am. I also ask him to return a signed copy by noon. He looks down at the table; I can see the shame on his face.

Not a single cell within me rejoices at his pain or misery. I don't even wonder if he has learned anything from being dishonest or the childish games he's played—I just pray he finds peace and comes to know the Universe as I am discovering it.

Frank asks me to order dinner and stay so we can discuss 2012. I agree, knowing I will not continue under the same arrangement or in the same capacity. *I must clearly communicate this.*

We talk for another hour—a quick meeting, considering how most of them go. I tell Frank I'd take on the new role he requests: creating and leading a division to develop and incubate new business strategies to fuel growth, moving away from business lines that appear to be fragile. My mind begins to race with the terms and words I need in my contract—and I rein it in. *"That's for another day,"* I coach myself. For now, just listen to what he wants—see if I am willing to give it to him.

I send Karen a quick update in the morning after I send the payment schedule to Frank. I owe Greg a phone call. My heart goes out to him. *Maybe he is thinking he can avoid Frank burnout. Maybe he wants a challenge.* Obviously I'll continue to support him while I begin to incubate the new division.

"I sense Frank is committed to the new division but part of me wonders for how long," I summarize to Karen. "All I want is to have clarity in whatever role I play, assuming I stay."

"Jim, it seems obvious to me the Universe has given you a ticket to ride," Karen responds.

"I like the sound of that," I chime in. "Ride what?" is the question I ask her.

"You have already declared you don't want to ride the crazy train any more, correct?"

"Absolutely," I affirm.

"And you know you want to work with companies and leadership that want authentic sustainable change?"

"It's what I am good at. I want to help business leaders understand that until you can manage yourself, you can't manage a business!"

I feel my passion engaging.

"So why doesn't Frank become a client? You have a few other small clients, but if you work on a contract you can perfect the value vs. time principle we have discussed. It's a perfect way to go out on your own—with a client who knows the quality of work you do."

"That would be perfect, but, Karen, I hear the 'how?' question popping up already though." Before she can comment I add, "But I'm not hooked by the how. Like someone wise once told me, "Just commit to your practice and let the game come to you."

"I agree, that is a wise person indeed," Karen laughs.

Within a few weeks I have my new contractor agreement with Frank. I also have my first payment on my bonus. I'm engaged from a creative aspect. Secretly, I wonder *if they have the discipline to truly sustain the growth I envision—but that isn't my part to take care of. My part is to fully express the possibilities, define a repeatable and scalable road map for them and keep moving my life forward.*

As summer morphs from spring before my eyes, I'm meeting more and more people who want and need my help. "Balance and Flow," Karen reminds me. "Let it develop organically. It's not like one day you will wave a magic wand and say 'Oh, I have a new life!' It's one day you look back and realize you do have a new life and it has come gracefully."

I'm also getting frequent questions about the book I've been telling everyone I am writing. The truth is, writing is hard work. Between family, marriage, basketball coaching, and work there isn't much time. Not to mention the curve balls of monkey-mind. It's time for my annual review and I'm hoping Karen will have some guidance for me. She has already taken the first part of the book and in essence said, "Here is what I witnessed you go through and what you'd say if you weren't consulting your monkey-mind," and re-written it. I really like what she did with my manuscript and tell her so.

"A ghost-writer can interview you, Jim, take your manuscript thus far and re-work it. I think you'll learn many lessons in the process," Karen smiles her all-knowing smile.

"I know this is asking a lot of you, Karen, but hear me out: I want you to do it—all of it. If you think about it—it makes perfect sense." I want to sell her on the idea, although I know that selling her is impossible. Still, I feel compelled to communicate clearly. "I'll work with your schedule, and no one besides me knows my journey to find the better way then you do."

"Jim, it's an interesting idea," Karen pauses. "I'm going to consider it and ask for guidance. You know I have never ghost written before, right?"

"Someone wise once told me something is only impossible until it's not," I say proudly.

Karen smiles, and says she'd let me know. A week later I have a thoughtful email from her outlining how we could work together on the book. It is a no brainer. Trust. We'll both move in Trust towards completion, surrendering along the way as to what to include and what to leave out.

Twelve months later, you have my journey in your hands as you read this.

As we finished, Karen asked me over coffee, the same question she asked the day we met: "What exactly is success, Jim?" Ahh, success, I remember this question well. This time I had an answer and without hesitating, I replied:

"Success for me is measured by peace and happiness.
It's showing up and being the person I want to be on a daily basis.
It begins with my spiritual relationship with God.
It's about being the kind of husband my wife would marry again,
the father my kids are proud to introduce their friends to,
the leader others want to follow,
and the kind of man I would want as a friend.
To me, that is SUCCESS!"

Karen smiled.

I can't tell you what will happen next in my life, nor do I want to limit the Universe by trying to predict the events to come. I can only testify to my life thus far in one sentiment,

"THERE IS A BETTER WAY."

ABOUT THE AUTHOR

Jim Riviello has dedicated his life to inspiring business people to re-imagine, re-focus and re-invent their leadership legacy.

He wrote *There Must Be a Better Way* and founded the Leadership X University to help business leaders drive clarity and discipline around the strategic growth components required to enable sustainable change—for themselves and their business.

Jim is a highly sought after expert on transformational change, business innovation and leadership development. He has spearheaded enterprise sales organizations, facilitated rapid growth as a C-level executive, and been a management consultant to Fortune 1000 companies. He has also launched and managed several successful startup organizations and nurtured them into profitable venues.

Jim has a passion for excellence, enormous energy and the ability to energize others. He authors a leadership blog www.jimriviello.com/blog where he openly shares the coveted lessons learned from his own path to success along with the additional ideas, tips and strategies he has collected from the highly successful individuals he has the privilege to work with on a daily basis.

Learn more about Jim at www.JimRiviello.com

33599498R00096

Made in the USA
Lexington, KY
30 June 2014